From Nyet to Da

INTERCULTURAL PRESS
A Nicholas Brealey Publishing Company

YARMOUTH, ME • BOSTON • LONDON

The InterAct Series

Other books in the series:

Also by Yale Richmond

From Nyet to Da
THIRD EDITION

Understanding the Russians

YALE RICHMOND

INTERCULTURAL PRESS, INC.

First published by Intercultural Press, a Nicholas Brealey Publishing Company, in 1992. Revised in 1996 and 2003. For information, contact:

Intercultural Press, Inc.
374 U.S. Route One
PO Box 700
Yarmouth, ME 04096, USA
Tel: 207-846-5168
Fax: 207-846-5181
www.interculturalpress.com

Nicholas Brealey Publishing
3–5 Spafield Street
Clerkenwell
London, EC1R 4QB, UK
Tel: +44-207-239-0360
Fax: +44-207-239-0370
www.nbrealey-books.com

Book design and production by Patty J. Topel

Printed in the United States of America

09   08   07   06   05   3   4   5   6   7

Library of Congress Cataloging-in-Publication Data

Richmond, Yale, 1923-
    From nyet to da: understanding the Russians / Yale Richmond.—3rd. ed.
        p. cm.—(InterAct Series)
    Includes bibliographical references and index.
    ISBN 1-877864-16-1
        1. Russian (Federation). 2. National characteristics. Russian. 3. Social psychology—Russia (Federation). 4. Russia (Federation)—Social life and customs. I. Title. II. Series.
    DK510.23.R53 2003
    947.085—dc21   20022038787

To all foreign advisers and volunteers who are giving so generously of their time to assist in the postcommunist transition in Russia and the other republics of the former Soviet Union.

Contents

I have never met anyone who understood Russians.

—Grand Duke Aleksandr Mihailovich

ARCTIC OCEAN

Bering
Sea

Alaska
(U.S.)

Kolyma

Lena

S S I A

Yenisey

Lena

Lake
Baikal

Amur

Amur

SAKHALIN
ISLAND

KURIL
ISLANDS

MONGOLIA

Vladivostok

NORTH
KOREA

SOUTH
KOREA

JAPAN

CHINA

Preface to the Third Edition

The Cold War has ended, communism has collapsed, and Russia's relations with the West have warmed. Russians are traveling abroad more freely, and foreign visitors are finding that distant land with its newly found freedoms a more pleasant place to visit. Russia and the West are learning that they have more to gain from cooperation than confrontation, but Russia still remains distant, separated from the West by culture, language, history, and misunderstandings.

Russia is no longer a superpower, though it is still a great power with which the West must seek cooperation on a wide variety of issues ranging from terrorism to arms control. Russia, for its part, needs foreign investment and Western know-how. Joint ventures find willing partners, but doing business with the Russians can still be burdensome as long-held patterns of behavior continue to be influenced by geography, history, and culture. Understanding the Russians—the theme of this book—remains a challenge.

This edition has been revised and updated to cover events and changes occurring in Russia since the first edition was published in 1992. Russia is indeed changing, but most of the Russians whom foreign visitors may encounter will still show many of the traits described here and in earlier editions. Differences may be seen between city dwellers and rural people, among the intelligentsia, workers, and peasants, and between generations, but they all share common characteristics, which will be described in these pages.

There are no shortcuts to understanding the Russians. It helps to know their language, history, and literature and to have worked with them over the years. Although not intended as a quick fix, this book has been written for readers without previous experience in Russian affairs who will be interacting with Russians in the coming years—business executives, government officials, advisers and consultants, scholars, scientists, and students as well as ordinary citizens.

The book is based on my more than twenty-five years of working with Russians—negotiating and facilitating people-to-people exchanges in culture, education, and science—when relations were good and when they were not. Those years include duty at the American Embassy in Moscow, numerous visits to the Soviet Union and Russia, and many years in Washington with the Department of State, United States Information Agency, Commission on Security and Cooperation in Europe (U.S. Congress), and National Endowment for Democracy.

When I first began to interact with Russians in the early 1960s, they had a well-earned reputation for being difficult. This was due, in part, to the Cold War mentality of the time, on both sides. But another, more fundamental factor was the inability of Americans and Russians to understand certain patterns of each other's behavior. This has led many to wonder why Russians are in some ways so similar to Americans and in others, so different.

There are risks, admittedly, in attempting to define national characteristics. A nation may be unfairly stereotyped, and there will always be exceptions to the rule. But who will not agree that Russians differ from Poles, Poles from Germans, and Germans from the French, although these nations have lived side by side in Europe from time immemorial? And Russians today in the Commonwealth of Independent States, as the successor to the Soviet Union is known, are recognizably different from Armenians, Georgians, and Moldovans, and even more different from Azeris, Kazakhs, and Uzbeks.

The Russian character, formed over centuries from unique experiences and traditions, has made Russians different from other Europeans as well as from Americans. Old traditions continue despite the revolutions of 1917 and seventy years of communism and will continue to influence whatever state and society evolve during the early years of the twenty-first century.

As the French historian François Guizot has written, looking back on his own country's revolutions:

> When nations have existed for a long and glorious time, they cannot break with their past, whatever they do; they are influenced by it at the very moment when they work to destroy it; in the midst of the most glaring transformations they remain fundamentally in character and destiny such as their history has formed them. Even the most daring and powerful revolutions cannot abolish national traditions of long duration. Therefore, it is most important, not only for the sake of intellectual curiosity but also for the good management of international relations, to know and to understand these traditions. (in Kohn 1955, vii)

Or, as *The New York Times* put it, "Russia's leaders are different, it's the people who are the same" (6 January 2002).

Acknowledgments

This edition has benefited from comments and suggestions on earlier editions received from many readers, both Russian and American. Particularly encouraging have been the favorable and complimentary letters received from Russians who do not understand how others perceive them. As one Russian writer, the author of many books about other cultures written for Russian readers, has said, "Throughout my life as a writer, I have been taking literary 'snapshots' of other people, and now someone has taken a snapshot of me. It is very revealing."

I am also indebted to David Johnson and his *Johnson's Russia List*, an Internet listserve that has been a valuable resource for facts, figures, and commentary on contemporary Russia.

In transliterating Russian names and words I have made some minor changes in the usual methods in order to more closely approximate the Russian pronunciation. Where another spelling has become accepted usage in English, I have followed the more familiar form.

—Yale Richmond
Washington, D.C.

Introduction

Many an American has returned from a first visit to Russia ex-
claiming, "I don't understand why we have had such difficulties
with the Russians. They're just like us." Subsequent visits—and a
closer look—will reveal that Russians and Americans do indeed
have differences. As a Russian journalist once told me, "Americans will at first see the similarities between our two peoples,
but they should also look for the differences."

This book will seek to explain those differences and to help
Americans understand why Russians behave like Russians. In
the process some readers may also learn why they behave like
Americans.

The surface similarities are readily apparent. Russians feel
a common identity with Americans as citizens of multiethnic,
continental great powers. In history, both peoples have been
expansionist. Americans moved west from the Atlantic coast
across the Great Plains and the Rocky Mountains to the Pacific
shores. Russians expanded in all directions but mostly east beyond
the Ural Mountains and across the vast stretches of Siberia to
the Pacific shores, and beyond to Alaska in 1741. Russians and

Americans eventually met in 1812 in California, where so many new overtures seem to occur.

Both tamed a wilderness. Indeed, as Russian and American historians have noted, there is a frontier spirit shared by Siberia and the American West. The landowning gentry and the bonded serf of European Russia were not common to Siberia, which was settled by such diverse groups as Cossacks, political and religious dissidents, independent peasants, runaway serfs, and exiled convicts. Today's residents of the Siberian metropolis Novosibirsk liken it to Chicago, which they know, by reputation, as a hustling, bustling city serving a vast hinterland. And both Russians and Americans regard themselves as chosen nations with a messianic mission, destined to bring their own versions of enlightenment to less fortunate people.

America and Russia today are also nuclear powers with the capacity to destroy each other and the rest of the world as well. Likewise, both face the challenges of reducing their awesome arsenals of armaments and coping with the environmental consequences of their weapons industries.

Americans and Russians also think big. Both are energetic and inventive. Russians appreciate the casual, direct, and often blunt American way of speaking, which they liken to their own—without pretense and different from the West European manner, which they find too formal, indirect, and less sincere. Finally, Russians, despite their traditional suspicion of foreigners, show heartfelt hospitality to visitors from abroad, a trait they share with Americans.

Differences between Russians and Americans are equally apparent. Authority in America, as Alexis de Tocqueville observed, has been diffused and flows upward from the people to a representative government. In Russia, authority has always been centralized and flows down. Pressure for change in the United States has come from below, and elected officials have either responded or eventually been replaced. Change in Russia has been imposed from above, and Russians have usually resisted because change there has been associated with hardship and misfortune.

In the United States, individuals are celebrated, and their rights vis-à-vis government are protected in both law and practice. In Russia, from its earliest years, individual rights have been subordinated to the greater communal good. In the U.S., pluralism and tolerance for diverse views prevail. Such diversity appears chaotic to Russians, who value consensus and a single prevailing truth. The American economy is based in the private sector and a free market, and the role of government has been minor. Russian governments, whether tsarist, communist, or postcommunist, have distrusted the free market and have played an active role in the economy. America's cultural roots are in Western Europe. Russia's roots are in both Europe and Asia, and historians still debate which has played the greater role in shaping the Russian character.

Historical experience also separates Russians and Americans. For much of its history Russia has been in a state of almost constant warfare with neighboring nations, and its people have often suffered extreme cruelties and violence in their own land. Since the Civil War, the United States has fought its wars mostly abroad, and its people have not known wartime hardship and devastation.

Whether similar or dissimilar, the two countries were thrust upon the world stage in the latter half of the twentieth century as nuclear superpowers and forced, rather reluctantly, to interact with each other. Only belatedly have they discovered the many common concerns they share, the most vital of which is the preservation of peace in the nuclear age.

Those weighty concerns, however, have not always led to improved understanding. Contact between Russians and Americans in the past has been limited, separated as the two peoples have been by distance, ideology, and language. Today, however, they are interacting to an extent never before anticipated, and the need for improved understanding has become urgent, not merely for a few diplomats and businesspeople but for all Americans and Russians.

Examples of misunderstanding abound. After World War II

xxiv

the United States, unaware of the extent of the Soviet Union's devastation and losses, feared a Soviet assault on Western Europe. The Russians, in turn, regarded U.S. economic and military assistance to Western Europe as a threat to their own security. Their field of vision narrowed by ideological blinders, they confidently awaited the collapse of capitalism and the triumph of what they called socialism. With the onset of the Cold War, paranoia grew on both sides.

The Cuban Missile Crisis of 1962, which brought the two superpowers to the brink of nuclear warfare, was the most frightful example of misjudgment. More recently, glasnost and perestroika were seen by some Americans as the start of a campaign to bring democracy to the Soviet Union. Other Americans, however, saw them as public relations gambits designed to deceive the West. More recently, as a new Russian president has shown an increasingly cooperative attitude toward the West, there are some who argue that Russia is no longer a great power and is irrelevant in international affairs. Clearly, the gap in understanding still exists.

To help bridge that gap and enable readers to better understand the new Russia that is now evolving, this book will focus on those forces that have shaped Russian behavior—geography, history, religion, culture, and governance—and how they differ from those that have formed American behavior.

The terms *Russian* and *Soviet* were often used interchangeably by both Russians and Americans (as they will be here occasionally). Even Soviet leaders at times incorrectly referred to the Soviet Union as Russia, although Russia as a sovereign state ceased to exist in 1922 when it became the Union of Soviet Socialist Republics. And in December 1991, reflecting the discrediting of communism and the increased sovereignty of the republics, the Soviet Union was transformed into a Commonwealth of Independent States, a loose political alliance whose permanence may also be questioned.

Our subject here will be the Russians rather than all of the more than one hundred nationalities that constituted the

Soviet people. While Russians numbered little more than half the population of the former Soviet Union, the political and economic leadership was almost entirely Russian, as were the top echelons of the Communist Party, armed forces, and KGB. Russian, moreover, was the predominant language and culture.

Whether Russian or Soviet, many changes have been occurring in that distant land which Winston Churchill in 1939 described as a riddle, wrapped in a mystery, inside an enigma. Today, we know much more about that riddle, but each day the media record events that no one, including Russians, could have foreseen only a few years ago. Russia is less of a mystery, but the enigma remains.

The nature of the recent changes can legitimately be questioned—are they real, and how long will they last? But whatever the results of Russia's most recent effort to modernize, change there will continue to be shaped by the Russian character, and that character, formed over a millennium, has changed slowly.

Russia was communist for seventy years but has been Russian Orthodox for a thousand, and Russians have lived even longer with their harsh climate, vast expanse of forest and steppe, and geographic and cultural isolation. To understand the Russians, one must know from whence they come.

Welcome to Moscow

My plane to Moscow was late, arriving in the dark at Sheremetyevo Airport on a winter evening a number of years ago after a
long flight from New York City. It was not a warm welcome. The
wind was bitter cold as passengers deplaned and piled aboard a
bus with frosted-over windows for the short ride to the terminal.
I had been traveling since the previous evening and was tired.

Inside the terminal the wait at immigration was long and
tedious as young, grim-faced border guards took their time checking passports and visas. The customs clearance was equally long
and thorough, but at last I was cleared and once more admitted
to Russia.

Russian airport terminals are crowded, noisy, and chaotic as
passengers mill about seeking friends and greeters. As elsewhere
in the East, airport arrivals and departures bring out throngs of
relatives and well-wishers, but not for me. Alone with my lug-
gage, I struggled to the head of the taxi line.

After a thirty-minute drive to the city and a hassle with the
taxi driver—Russia's most zealous capitalists—who wanted to be
paid in dollars, I arrived at the Ukraina. Unlike Moscow's newer
hotels, the old Ukraina was built in the "wedding cake" style of
the Stalin era and had a musty decor that reminded a visitor of
old Russia. I first stayed at the hotel in 1963 and over the years
had become accustomed to its shabby and faded inelegance.

There was no line at the registration desk, just the usual

crowd, pushing, shoving, and trying to get the attention of the lone clerk. After a fifteen-minute wait, I finally registered, gave my bags to a porter, showed my hotel identification card to the ever present guard who admitted me to the inner lobby, and was on my way to an upper floor. One final hassle occurred before I was settled in my room—the porter demanded to be tipped in dollars or with a pack of Marlboros (the preferred brand in Russia).

It was then that hunger hit. I had not eaten since a light lunch on my flight and was looking forward to a snack at the hotel *bufet*, a sort of Russian snack bar. But to eat at the bufet I first had to change dollars into rubles, since Soviet currency in those years could not legally be brought into the Soviet Union.

Making my way down the long dim hall, I approached the *dyezhurnaya* (person on duty) for my floor. A feature of many Russian hotels, they are the women who keep the keys, control access to rooms, and provide hot water for tea or instant coffee. Inquiring about the location of the currency exchange office, I was told that it had closed for the day.

"*Shto delat?*" (What to do?), I asked.

Shrugging her shoulders, she looked me over indifferently. Here was the making of a classic confrontation between a Western visitor and the Soviet system, which was not designed to serve individuals with special requests. Had I been a member of a tour group, there would have been a guide to tend to my needs, and dinner would have been planned for the group at the hotel restaurant, paid in advance, and there would have been no need to change money. But here I was, a lone traveler who had to get something to eat before falling into bed to catch up with the eight-hour time change from New York.

From past experience in Russia I knew not to retreat, so I stood my ground, changed the subject, and began to converse with the old woman. We talked about my long trip from the States, the purpose of my visit, the Moscow weather, where I had learned to speak Russian, the current shortages in Moscow, her children and mine, and how nice it was for me to be back in Russia again. After a while, I returned to the subject of my hunger and asked if she had any suggestions as to what I might do before the snack bar closed for the night.

"I'll lend you some rubles," she replied, reaching for her *sumka* (satchel) under the desk, "and you can pay me back tomorrow."

My approach had worked. A kind Russian grandmother had taken pity on a hungry American and lent him a few of her own rubles so he could get some *khleb, sir, i chai* (bread, cheese, and tea) before retiring for the night. Welcome to Moscow!

The lesson of this story—and this book—is simple. Russia can be a cold and impersonal place, where a visitor's requests all too often meet with an automatic *nyet*. But Russians respond to a human approach, and they can be warm and helpful once a good interpersonal relationship has been established. When that point is reached, their word is good, *nyet* becomes *da*, and deals can be done. That is the key to understanding the Russians.

Geography and Culture

All civilizations are to some extent the product of geographical factors, but history provides no clearer example of the profound influence of geography upon a culture than in the historical development of the Russian people.

—George Vernadsky, *A History of Russia*

The Origins of Russia

One Rus has its roots in a universal, or at least European, culture. In this Rus the ideas of goodness, honor and freedom are understood as in the West. But there is another Rus: the Rus of the dark forests, the Rus of the Taiga, the animal Russia, the fanatic Russia, the Mongol-Tatar Russia. This last Russia made despotism and fanaticism its ideal.... Kievan Rus was a part of Europe, Moscow remained the negation of Europe.

—Leo Tolstoy

Former President Mikhail Gorbachev, in 1989, endorsed the concept of a "common European home," with Russia as a tenant. In geographic terms the common European home makes sense. Europe does extend from the Atlantic Ocean to the Ural Mountains, and Russia—at least a part of it—is indeed in Europe. But through much of its history, Russia has been isolated

5

6

from or has rejected Europe and its Western ways. Gorbachev's common European home, with Russia occupying the back porch and the United States and Canada the front porch, was a new concept in geopolitical real estate.

The great rivers of Russia flow north and south, and along those rivers came Russia's early contacts with the outside world. From the northern rivers in the ninth century came Viking raiders and traders from Scandinavia who became the rulers of Rus, the city-principality of Kiev and the forerunner of the Russian state. From the southern rivers came contacts with Byzantium, the Eastern half of the Christian Roman Empire, and its resplendent capital, the Greek city of Constantinople (today's Istanbul), whence came Russia's religion, law, and art.

Kievan Rus converted to Orthodox Christianity in 988, and Constantinople became its link to the Mediterranean and the West for commerce as well as culture. But scarcely a century later that linkage was threatened by repeated onslaughts of mounted marauders from Asia moving westward over the great Eurasian steppe. When those invaders reached the Kievan Rus state and threatened its capital, the Rus began to migrate north, seeking protection in remote forests inhabited at that time by Finnish tribes. Power gradually shifted from Kievan Rus to Russian Muscovy.

The Mongols (called Tatars in early Russian sources) invaded Russia in the mid-thirteenth century.[*] Unstoppable, they took Moscow in 1234 and Kiev in 1240 and made Russian princes their vassals for the next two hundred years. While the Mongol-Tatar conquest did not make Asians of the Russians, it did delay their becoming Europeans. It also produced today's Russians—a mixture of Slavic, Finnish, and Tatar blood.

When Moscow liberated itself from the Tatar yoke in 1480, the modern Russian state was born. Distant from Europe, the new

---

[*] The Mongols were a Mongolian people; the Tatars were Turkic. But as the Mongol empire expanded, it encompassed more and more Turkic peoples. Hence the Russian use of *Tatar* for *Mongol*.

state was cut off from Constantinople, which in 1453 had fallen to the Muslim Ottoman Turks. The Russian Orthodox Church, isolated from the rest of Christianity, developed independently as a national church.

Moscow, moreover, saw itself as the third and last Rome, successor to Rome and Constantinople, the two capitals of the Roman Empire, which in turn had fallen to barbarians and infidels. Russia was regarded by its religious and lay leaders as a holy land with an imperial mission, a new center of Christianity, destined to unite the peoples of East and West. It was at that time that Russian rulers began to use the title tsar, derived from the Latin *Caesar*.

Russia's historic distrust of the West has its roots in that religious schism and its aftermath. Remote from the West, Russia experienced none of the major developments that shaped modern Europe—the Renaissance with its revival of classical influence and flowering of the arts, the Reformation with its pluralism of religious and secular thought, the rise of big cities, the development of modern agriculture and commerce, the scientific revolution, economic liberalism and recognition of individual rights, the beginnings of political liberty, and the growth of a strong middle class. In the West the middle class was in the forefront of reform. Russia's failure to develop a strong middle class delayed reform.

Cut off from the West, Russia remained a vast, backward, largely agricultural empire, regimented and ruled by an autocratic dynasty with a holy mission to defend its faith against the barbarians of the East and the heresies and pluralism of the West.

The pluralism of the West, moreover, was seen by Russia as chaotic, a cacophony of voices without harmony, a disunity of thought and purpose. To that West Russia would nevertheless come during its periodic attempts to modernize, seeking science, technology, and administrative know-how but rejecting at the same time the Western ways that came with the modernization it so sorely needed.

To remote Russia, many things Western have come late—

manufacturing, higher education, science and technology, the management sciences, and computers as well as blue jeans and rock music. Other things Western have not yet arrived—good government, transparency, and efficiency. These come from a West that Russia has openly disdained but secretly envied and from which it is today again trying to learn.

The Cold North

> The aim of civilization in the North is serious. There, society is the fruit, not of human pleasures, not of interests and passions easily satisfied, but of a will ever persisting and ever thwarted which urges the people to incomprehensible efforts. There, if individuals unite together, it is to struggle with a rebellious nature, which unwillingly responds to the demands made upon her.
> —Marquis de Custine, *Empire of the Czar*

Mention the Russian winter and most people will think of deep snow, piled to the rooftops. Actually, the snow is not that deep in Russia, and winter is known more for its frigid temperatures, which Russians find invigorating. They break out their winter clothing and cross-country skis and appear to enjoy the below-freezing weather. Those temperatures, however, can become unbearable when the wind blows across the open land and the windchill factor plummets.

Russia is a northern country. Moscow lies on the same latitude as the lower Hudson Bay. Russia's northernmost port, Murmansk, is further north than Nome, Alaska. Its most southern port, Novorossisk, on the Black Sea, is on the same latitude as Minneapolis.

Nature has not been kind to Russia. Much of European Russia and Siberia is very cold much of the year. Permafrost covers 59 percent of its territory, which limits the availability of farmland. Autumn is brief and followed by a long and cold winter. Summers are short and hot. In Old Russia, where the economy was mostly agricultural, peasants could do little during the winter months, and they more or less hibernated, holed up in their huts, seeking to survive while awaiting spring and the sowing season.

When spring did arrive, there was much to be done, all in a short span of time. In Russia's northern lands, there are fewer than five months from spring, when the ground can be tilled and seeded, until fall, when crops must be harvested before the first frost. During those precious few months, Russians over the centuries have worked almost around the clock to produce the food needed to get them through the following winter.

According to one popular theory, this explains why Russians often appear inactive for long periods of time and then show intense bursts of energy. The stagnation of the Brezhnev era, for example, can be seen as a long winter of hibernation, and the perestroika of the Gorbachev years, as a short spring and summer of frenzied effort.

The harsh climate also explains the strength of Russians, their ability to endure extreme hardship, and their bleak outlook on life as well as their patience and submission. Climate has also made them cautious. In Russia's farmlands weather is often unpredictable and crop failure an ever present possibility. In an agricultural society where survival depends on the weather, it is imprudent to take chances. And as in all traditional societies, the test of time is preferred to the risks of the new and untried.

Does climate still make a difference in the early years of the twenty-first century? Over millennia, people everywhere have adapted to their environment, and today some have even tamed it. Americans, with central heating, air conditioning, and other modern conveniences, have literally insulated themselves from weather's extremes. American culture and character today are not much different in Minnesota than from states with milder climes.

Russians, however, have been living in their cold north for millennia, and for much of that time as serfs and peasants in a primitive agricultural society. Until recently, most Russians have lived much as their ancestors did before them—in small villages, distant and isolated, their freedom of movement restricted, and without the comforts and labor-saving tools provided by modern society. The cold north is still very much in their bones and psyches.

A Russian winter has to be lived through to be really appreciated. Winter starts in October and continues through March, with November to January being the darkest months. St. Petersburg, at the winter solstice, has only five and one-half hours of daylight, and on days with overcast skies and smog there is often no sun to be seen. In the Russian far north during the dead of winter, the sun never rises at all.†

During the winter months, many Russians suffer from Seasonal Affective Disorder (SAD), as the ailment is known in the West. Anger, hostility, fatigue, and depression increase as does the demand for psychiatric services. Vodka consumption rises, alcoholic treatment centers overflow, and suicides rise. Hundreds of homeless die of hypothermia. Political discontent reaches its peak.

Distance and Isolation

> Forced to withdraw into the northeastern corner of Europe and to use all their strength there in the difficult labor of national unification, the Russian people found themselves, from the thirteenth century on, physically separated from the rest of the Christian world.
>
> —S. M. Solovyov, *Peter's Reforms*

Most countries have only one time zone. The United States has six, and Americans in the eastern part of the country who watch a football game in California know that there is a three-hour time difference. Russia, however, has eleven time zones and is almost twice as large as the U.S., stretching six thousand miles from

---

† In summer, by contrast, the days are long, and in the Russian North, it never gets dark at night. During St. Petersburg's *Byeliye Nochi* (White Nights) in the last two weeks of June, the sun barely dips below the horizon.

west to east. A trip from Moscow to Vladivostok on the Pacific via the famous Trans-Siberian Railway, extending over more than one-third of the globe's circumference, takes seven days.

This vast landmass—one-eighth of the earth's land surface—has only limited access to world oceans. Moreover, Russia's natural resources are mostly in Siberia and the Arctic region, far from the markets and population centers of European Russia. Denied cheap water transport, Russia has had to depend on expensive and difficult-to-maintain surface transport over long distances. Deep in its Eurasian remoteness, Russia has been distant from Europe, the Mediterranean, the Middle East, China, and other great centers of civilization. Moscow is some three thousand miles from Paris, and before the age of the railroad, such an arduous journey could take as long as six weeks.

The two momentous events mentioned earlier—the Mongol-Tatar invasions of the thirteenth century, which cut Russia off from Europe for almost 250 years, and the fall of Constantinople (the center of Eastern Christianity) to the Turks in 1453—caused Russia's commercial, cultural, and religious isolation and retarded its development for centuries, a handicap it has never fully overcome.

Distance and isolation also deterred development of a mercantile tradition. Self-sufficient in agriculture and natural resources and with no great need to trade with other countries, Russia became inwardly oriented. Contacts with the outside world were through neighboring states, and when conflicts arose with those states, they were often resolved by military force, resulting in the absorption of more and more new lands.

Geography also made Russia vulnerable to wars—literally hundreds of them—along her lengthy borders which have no natural defenses. To the east, the great Eurasian steppe served as a highway for waves of invaders from Asia who, in ancient times, repeatedly swept into Russia. From the west, Russia has been invaded by Teutonic Knights, Lithuanians, Poles, Swedes, the French, and Germans. And to the south, Russia has had continuous wars over the centuries with Turkic tribes.

As a result of that constant border warfare, Russia became the largest state—actually an empire—on earth. Its expansion, moreover, resulted in even longer undefined borders as well as heightened suspicion of neighboring nations.

With such a vast territory to govern, Russia evolved into a state ruled from its center and organized along paramilitary lines. Service to the state was a duty for both nobles and peasants. Surrounded by hostile powers, Russia became dependent on the use of force in its relations with neighboring states and obsessed with security—traits that still survive. Although the Mongols invaded Russia some seven hundred years ago, the memory of their rule is one reason for Russia's deep-rooted suspicion of China today. But that fear is perhaps understandable, considering the more than one billion Chinese on the other side of an indefensible and oft-contested border and a vast and relatively empty Siberia, rich in resources. Visitors to Russia should avoid making comparisons with China, which can provoke visceral reactions among Russians.

How has a state ringed by so many adversaries been able to continually extend its territorial reach? As Russians see it, they have been victims of foreign aggression, and Russia's expansion is the result of victories over foreign invaders. As others see it, Russia has taken advantage of weakness or instability in neighboring states to annex territories along her periphery.

One sharp critic of Russian territorial aggrandizement in the mid-nineteenth century was a London-based correspondent of the *New York Tribune* named Karl Marx. In 1852, in his coverage of events leading to the Crimean War, Marx wrote:

> Russia's acquisitions from Sweden are greater than what remains of that kingdom; from Poland, nearly equal to the Austrian empire; from Turkey in Europe, greater than Prussia (exclusive of the Rhenish provinces); from Turkey in Asia, as large as the whole dominion of Germany proper; from Persia, equal to England; from Tartary, to an extent as large as European Turkey, Greece, Italy, and Spain, taken together. The total acquisitions of Russia

during the last sixty years are equal in extent and importance to the whole Empire she had in Europe before that time. (in Henze 1987, 36)

Along with her territorial expansion, Russia sought protection from foreign influence. Periodic attempts to introduce European technology and Western ways met with the sullen resistance of most of the Russian people. Suspicion and mistrust of foreigners—and the West in particular—have been a recurring theme in both Russian and Soviet history, and the Iron Curtain of the Soviet era was its most recent manifestation. New ideas have come late to Russia, when they have come at all.

The United States has also been a continental power and expansionist, but with a maritime and commercial tradition. The Atlantic and Pacific Oceans served as natural defenses, providing protection from foreign aggression and ensuring the peace necessary for economic development at home and trade abroad. The American fixation with freedom of the seas can be compared with Russia's obsession with security along her borders. The objective of both countries has been to ensure stability and well-being at home.

The United States' commercial experience and Russia's lack of a mercantile tradition have given the two countries different world outlooks. As Harvard's Richard Pipes points out: "Commerce is...by its very nature conducive to compromise. Nations raised on it instinctively seek a common ground for agreement, that exact point at which the other side might be prepared to make a deal" (1981, 16). Compromise is native to America but alien to Russia.

The oceans, moreover, have been bridges for the United States, providing easy access to other countries and cultures. New ideas have usually been welcomed, or at least not opposed; and the oceans served as highways for waves of immigrants who came in peace and with hope, turning their backs on the rigid class divisions of the Old World to seek a better life in the New.

They brought vitality and talent to a constantly changing and dynamic society.

The New World is indeed new, only some four hundred years old, compared with Russia's more than one thousand. Russians, moreover, have been living in their native environment from time immemorial, and change has come slowly. The new has been welcomed in America, the old has been revered in Russia.

Communalism

[For Russians] the striving for corporate forms of activity has always prevailed over individualism.
                                    —Vladimir Putin, *First Person*

Sobornost (communal spirit, togetherness) distinguishes Russians from Westerners, for whom individualism and competitiveness are more common characteristics. As Nicolas Zernov put it, in Russia there is the desire "to find the balance between the conflicting outlooks of Europe and Asia, between Western claims to personal freedom and Oriental insistence on the integration of the individual into the community" (1978, 176).

Russia, writes Nina Khrushcheva, a granddaughter of Nikita Khrushchev,

had always valued the communal way of life over the merely individual. Community was seen so near to the ideal of brotherly love, which forms the essence of Christianity and thus represents the higher mission of the people. In this higher mission a commune—a triumph of human spirit—was understood as opposing law, formal organizations, and personal interests. (2000/2001, 48)

Russian communalism was not an invention of communists, although its traditions were exploited under the Soviets. The affinity for the group has deep roots in Russian culture, and its origins can be traced to the vastness of the great Russian plain.

In prehistoric times Russians banded together to fell the for-est, till the soil, harvest the crops, and protect themselves from invaders and marauders. Tools and weapons were primitive and life was harsh, but those handicaps could be overcome and sur-vival ensured—although just barely—by the collective effort of living and working together.

The *zadruga*, a clan or greater family commune, served as the nucleus of a tribal society. In time, it evolved into a larger unit, the *mir*, an agricultural village commune (also known as *obshchina*) based on territory and mutual interests. Member fami-lies lived in small hamlets, in huts side by side. The surrounding land was held in common by the mir and was unfenced. Each family, however, had its own hut, maintained a small plot of land for a family garden, and took its meals at home.[‡]

Land utilization was the mir's primary purpose and the basis for its survival. The mir determined how much of the common land each family would work, depending on its size and needs. It decided which crops would be grown and when they would be planted and harvested. It collected taxes and settled local disputes. The mir's authority, moreover, extended beyond land matters—it also disciplined members, intervened in family dis-putes, settled issues which affected the community as a whole, and otherwise regulated the affairs of its self-contained and isolated agricultural world.

The word *mir*, in fact, has three meanings in Russian—village commune, world, and peace—and for its members it symbolized all three. That little world of the Russian peasant—the bulk of the populace—was a world apart from, and at least a century behind, the lifestyles of landowners and city dwellers.

Decisions of the mir were made in a village assembly of heads

---

[‡] The idea of land held in common for the benefit of the community has ancient roots in many societies. In England it was custom-ary, before the Norman conquest and the introduction of private property. One relic today, in the heart of an American city, is the Boston Common.

16

of households. All members could speak and discussions were lively, but no vote was taken. The objective was to determine the collective will, and after an issue had been thoroughly discussed and opposition to it had ceased, a consensus evolved, which became binding on all households. Richard Stites describes the mir meetings as marked by "seemingly immense disorder and chaos, interruptions, and shouting; in fact it achieved business-like results" (1989, 124).

When peasants moved to cities as workers and craftsmen, they brought with them their communal way of life and formed workers' cooperatives called *artels*. Modeled on the mir, artel members hired themselves out for jobs as a group and shared the payments for their work. Some artels rented communal apartments where they would share the rent, buy the food, dine together, and even attend leisure events as a group. Hundreds of thousands of workers lived in this way in the generation or so before the Revolution (Stites, 207). In the city, as in the village, security and survival were ensured by a collective effort.

That communal way of life persisted well into the twentieth century, lasting longer in Russia than elsewhere in Europe. Tsarist Russia encouraged the mir because it served as a form of state control over the peasants and facilitated tax collection and military conscription. Because the mir affected so many people, and for such a long time, it played a major role in forming the Russian character. In the late 1950s, for example, when Soviet students began to come to the United States and were assigned in groups to American universities, they would often pool their stipends, live off a small part of their shared funds, and save as much as they could for later purchases.[§]

As Lev Tikhomirov—appropriately, with a *mir* in the middle of his name—wrote in 1888, "The Great Russian cannot imagine a life outside his society, outside the mir.... The Great Russian says: 'The mir is a fine fellow, I will not desert the mir. Even death is beautiful in common'" (in Miller 1961, 81).

[§] Related by Daniel Matuszewski, former IREX deputy director, in e-mail to author, 15 December 2001.

Serfdom (personal bondage) was imposed on most Russian peasants in the late sixteenth century and lasted for three hundred years before being abolished in 1861 (two years before slavery ended in the United States). The emancipation of serfs was accompanied by a land redistribution that enabled serfs, in principle, to purchase land outside the commune. However, land distributed under the reform was actually given to the mir, which held it in common until its members could make redemption payments.

That freed the serfs but preserved the mir, and peasants once more found themselves bound to the land they worked, since most of them were financially unable to leave the commune. The reform thus continued the mir's power over peasants and their submission to a higher authority which regulated the social order.

Service to the state also continued. The emancipation was accompanied by a reduction in the length of obligatory military service for former serfs and the lower class of townspeople. After 1861 the length of duty for those selected was reduced from twenty-five to sixteen years! A later reform in 1874 made military service compulsory for all able-bodied males over age twenty; the tour of active duty was further reduced to six years but was followed by nine years in the reserve and five more in the *militsia* (police).

The mir endured in various forms until the early 1930s, when it was replaced by yet another form of communal life, the Soviet collective farm. A modern-day effort by the state to tie peasants to the land, the brutally enforced collectivization was strongly opposed by the peasants, especially in Ukraine. The objective was to ensure an adequate supply of food for the cities, which were to grow under the industrialization of the Five-Year Plans. The immediate result, however, was famine and the death of millions in the countryside.

The contrast between Russian communalism and American individualism can best be seen in the differences between Russian peasants and American farmers. Agricultural settlers in the United States were independent farmers and ranchers who owned their own land and lived on it, self-sufficient and distant from their neighbors. In contrast to peasants of the mir, American farmers lived behind fences that marked the limits of their property. The Americans, moreover, were entrepreneurs in the sense that they managed their holdings individually, taking economic risks and regulating their own affairs, independent of the state.

The United States has also had its communes—and still has some today—an indication of some innate human urge to band and bond together. Those communes, however, have existed on the fringes of society rather than at its center. In the U.S. the commune is considered alien (unless Native Americans are taken into account); to Russians, it is native.

Individualism is esteemed in the West, but in Russian the word has a pejorative meaning. Steeped in the heritage of the mir, Russians think of themselves as members of a community rather than as individuals. Communal spirit helps to explain many of their characteristics—behavior in crowds, for example.

Physical contact with complete strangers—anathema to Americans and West Europeans—does not bother Russians. In crowds, they touch, push, shove, and even use elbows without hard feelings—except in the ribs of those who are competing with them to obtain access to something. Visitors to Russia should not take such pokes personally. Politeness takes different forms in different societies, and behavior in crowds can vary.

A crowd of passengers attempting to board a ship in Odessa in the early 1960s caught the attention of British traveler Laurens van der Post. A ship's officer stood on the quay collecting tickets at the gangway. The crowd pushed and jostled but never lost its temper. Although the people in the crowd shouted at the officer and elbowed him out of the way, he did not appear irritated, nor did he attempt to call them to order. A Russian friend related to van der Post how a group of French tourists, caught earlier in the same situation and annoyed by the crowd's persistent jostling, had lost their tempers and lashed out angrily at everyone near them. "The Russians were horrified at such lack of traveling manners," wrote van der Post, "presumably because it was personal retaliation and not the collective, impersonal pressure they were all applying to get through a bottleneck" (1965, 173). Foreign visitors who are averse to close contact should avoid the Moscow Metro during rush hours, 8:00 to 9:00 A.M. and 5:00 to 6:00 P.M.

Accustomed to close physical contact, Russian men as well as women touch when talking. Women dance with other women if there are not enough men to go around or if not asked by a man to dance. Russian men embrace and kiss each other, on the lips as well as cheeks, as I learned once when a male planted a kiss on my lips, much to my surprise, at the end of a long and festive evening. Americans are advised, however, not to initiate such spontaneous displays of affection, as President Jimmy Carter learned when he kissed Leonid Brezhnev (on the cheek) at their Vienna summit, much to Brezhnev's surprise and embarrassment.

Recreational activities are often arranged in groups, as in the artel. After working together all day, factory and office employees will spend evenings in group excursions to theaters and other cultural events organized by their shop stewards.

Russians seem compelled to intrude into the private affairs of others. Older Russians admonish young men and women—complete strangers—for perceived wrongdoings, using the patronizing term of address, *molodoy chelovek* (young man) or *dyevushka* (girl). On the streets, older women volunteer advice to young mothers on the care of their children. American parents in Moscow have been accosted by Russian women and accused of not dressing their children properly for the severe winter. One American, whose child was clad in well-insulated outerwear, would respond by unzipping her child's jacket and inviting the Russian women to feel how warm her child's body actually was. In a collective society, one's business is also everyone else's. (One intrusion that is both appreciated and expected is to inform others when they show the telltale white skin blotches that indicate the onset of frostbite.)

Russians do not hesitate to visit a friend's home without advance notice, even dropping in unexpectedly late at night as long as a light can be seen in a window. They routinely offer overnight accommodations to friends who are visiting their cities, a gesture based not only on their tradition of hospitality to travelers but also on the shortage of affordable overnight hotel accommodations. Americans who are accepted as friends by Russians will find that they too may receive unexpected visits and requests for lodging from their new friends.

Communism reinforced the Russian communal ethic but also added a coercive element, as illustrated by an *anekdot* (humorous story) about a schoolteacher who was lecturing her class on the virtues of *kollektivnost* (collective spirit).

"What did you do today, Ivan, to help your fellow citizens?" she asked.

"I helped an old lady to cross the street," replied Ivan.

"Very good," said the teacher, who turned to Boris and asked what he had done.

"I helped Ivan to help the old lady cross the street," answered Boris.

"Excellent," said the teacher, lauding their joint effort. "And Mikhail," she continued, "what did you do?"

"I helped Boris to help Ivan to help the old lady cross the street," said Mikhail.

"Splendid," exclaimed the teacher, pleased by their kollektivnost. "But why," she asked, "did it take three strong young boys to help one old lady to cross the street?"

"She didn't want to cross," replied the boys.

Nationality

Throughout Russian history one dominating theme has been the frontier; the theme of the struggle of the mastering of the resources of an untamed country, expanded into a continent by

the ever-shifting movement of the Russian people and their conquest of and intermingling with other peoples.
—B. H. Sumner, *A Short History of Russia*

No greater mistake can be made by a visitor to Russia than to assume that every Russian-speaking person encountered will be a Russian. The Russian Federation, the name of the new Russia, is a multinational state comprising people of many different nations whom, as British historian B. H. Sumner reminded us, the Russians conquered and intermingled with in their expansion throughout history.

The difference is nationality—the "nation" or ethnic group that an individual belongs to, which numbers some 176 in today's Russia. They include such people as Bashkirs, Buryats, Chechens, Chuvash, Ingush, Kalmyks, Komis, Mordvinians, Ossetians, Tatars, Yakuts, and many others, all with their own cultures and languages. Moreover, one of every seven Russian citizens, some twenty million, has an Islamic heritage. The birthrate among such families is much higher than that of ethnic Russians, a fact that concerns Russians as their own birthrate declines. Also of concern to Russians is the ethnic consciousness among some people and their desire for autonomy or self-rule.

Russia's territorial expansion began in the sixteenth century, and over the next three hundred years it annexed along its periphery—north, south, east, and west—lands with non-Russian peoples. How to deal with those nationalities in a vast empire ruled from its Russian center has been a challenge to Russian tsars, Soviet commissars, and now the elected leaders of the new Russia.

Throughout much of modern history, the Russians were a bare majority in their own country. That changed with the breakup of the Soviet Union, and today ethnic Russians number 82 percent of 145 million people of the Russian Federation.

Despite the loss of its peripheral lands, Russia today is still a vast state, extending from St. Petersburg (formerly Leningrad) to the Sea of Japan, retaining three-fourths of the territory of the former Soviet Union, with little more than half its population but with most of its natural resources—oil, gas, coal, gold, diamonds, and timber, among others.

Of the Russian Federation's eighty-nine administrative units, thirty-one are so-called autonomous entities, where most of the non-Russians live—sixteen autonomous republics, five autonomous regions, and ten autonomous districts. Together, these entities make up about half the area of the Russian Federation and contain most of its natural and mineral resources. In these "autonomies" Russian is the lingua franca, intermarriage with Russians is common, and the population has been heavily "Russified." In twenty-six of the thirty-one autonomies, Russians are in the majority.

In some autonomies, however, ethnic consciousness is high, as in Chechnya, a non-Slavic, largely Muslim republic in the Caucasus Mountains. Chechnya is the size of Connecticut and has a population of 1.2 million, of whom one million are Chechens. Russia brought the republic under its control and annexed it in 1864 after a bitter guerrilla war that lasted several decades. But nationalism remained high, and in 1944, during World War II, Joseph Stalin exiled the entire Chechen population to Soviet Central Asia, from which the survivors were allowed to return only some ten years later. In 1991, Chechnya declared its independence from the Russian Federation, and a civil war followed in which more than 100,000 Chechens and Russians were killed before a truce was finally signed in 1996. Despite several cease-fires, fighting resumed in 1999 and has continued as Russia once more sought to impose a military solution on a political problem.

The movement for autonomy or self-rule is also strong in areas with Russian majorities where local leaders seek increased independence and financial gain by loosening political and economic ties with the Moscow central government. Ethnic and local consciousness is on the rise in Russia, and people who interact with Russians and other ethnic groups should appreciate its significance.

Prior to its breakup in 1991, the Soviet Union had a population of 290 million and was the world's third most populous country, after China and India. Predominant were the three Slavic nations that speak related languages and share a common Christian heritage—Russians, with a little more than 50 percent of the Soviet population; Ukrainians, 18 percent; and Belarusians, 3.6 percent. Other major Soviet nationalities with a Christian heritage were Georgians and Armenians, 3 percent; Lithuanians, Latvians, and Estonians, 3 percent; and Moldovans, 1 percent.

Nations with an Islamic or Turkic heritage were another 20 percent of the Soviet population, with Azeri, Kazakh, Kyrgyz, Tatar, Tajik, Turkmen, and Uzbek being the major nationalities. And in the far north lived Arctic peoples with cultures similar to those of their North American cousins.

Nationality and religion are interrelated. Russians and Belarusians are Russian Orthodox. Ukrainians may be Ukrainian Autocephalous Orthodox, Russian Orthodox, or, in western Ukraine (which for centuries was a part of Poland), Ukrainian Catholic (Uniate), a church that uses the Eastern rite but is in union with the Roman Catholic Church in recognizing the authority of the Pope. Armenians and Georgians, who have their own churches, have been Christian since A.D. 301 and A.D. 318 respectively. Lithuanians are Roman Catholic by virtue of having been part of the Polish-Lithuanian Commonwealth for four centuries. Latvians and Estonians are Lutheran, a heritage of their German colonization and Swedish rule. Moldovans, like their fellow Romanians, are Orthodox.

Responding to the challenge of Zionism, the Soviet Union in 1928 established a Jewish Autonomous Region around Birobijan on the China border. Birobijan, however, has never attracted many Jews, and today they make up only 3 percent of the population.

Belarus and western Ukraine, as noted above, were under Polish rule from the fourteenth to the eighteenth centuries, and western portions of those lands were again a part of Poland between the two world wars. As a result, many Ukrainians and Belarusians appear more Western than do Russians. Ukraine, moreover, is located in a southern, more temperate zone and was known as the breadbasket of Russia and Europe. As "southerners," Ukrainians tend to be more outgoing and optimistic than their northern cousins.

The three Baltic republics were recognized as independent by Moscow in September 1991. All the other Soviet republics followed their lead in December but, as sovereign states, they chose to join the new Commonwealth of Independent States (CIS), which replaced the Soviet Union.

To further complicate this ethnic mosaic, some twenty million Russians live outside the Russian Federation in the other former Soviet republics, known as the "Near Abroad." There, they are a potential source of conflict with local governments, and the Russian Federation feels responsible for their welfare. In many parts of the Russian Federation there are also Germans, Poles, Jews, and other nationalities that do not have their own designated territories. Although interest in local languages has increased in recent years, Russian is still the lingua franca of the CIS, the language Uzbeks use to talk with Russians, and Armenians with Azeris (when they are talking to each other).

Americans also live in a multinational or multicultural state that has one dominant language, English, and culture, "Anglo." Americans may therefore find it difficult to comprehend the complexity of Russian nationality problems and to appreciate their political importance.

The difference lies in two almost contradictory aspects of American culture. One is America's role as a melting pot during its first 175 years of nationhood, absorbing waves of immigrants from many parts of Europe, who in time were assimilated into the dominant American culture. Within a few generations, the Old-World languages of the immigrants were largely lost, and cultural ties to the old country became mostly a matter of sentiment. In recent years, an influx of Latinos and Asians has created a large body of Americans who take pride in their cultural and linguistic diversity; Americans, however, recognize that their society is pluralistic, composed of different backgrounds and races, and they pride themselves on their ability to create unity in diversity.

In Russia, ethnic diversity is a completely different phenomenon, based on centuries of residence by various nationalities in their historic regions of origin and on the determination of many of them to preserve their distinct languages and cultures.

In Western and Central Europe, nationality as a political issue was largely resolved during the late nineteenth and early twentieth centuries. To be sure, the formation of new nation-states and the redrawing of national borders, particularly after World War I, did not impose perfect solutions. Nationality conflicts continue today in Belgium, Bulgaria, Italy, Romania, Slovakia, Spain, and the former Yugoslavia. But nationality differences have not threatened the existence of these states, Yugoslavia excepted.

In the East, however, nationalism and ethnicity have re-emerged in the 1990s to threaten the stability of several states. Centuries-old ethnic and national rivalries and passions have resurfaced and resulted in violence between non-Russian nationalities—Armenians and Azeris, Uzbeks and Mshkets, Georgians and Abkhazians, and Chechens and Ingush. Attempts at Russification by Moscow are resisted by some today as strongly as they were under the tsars and the Soviets.

In response to those ethnic stirrings, there has been a resurgence of Russian nationalism and a renewed interest in Russian Orthodoxy. Most Russians regret the breakup of the Soviet Union, and there is some Russian sentiment for a union of Russia with Ukraine and Belarus in a greater Slav state, including perhaps the northern half of Kazakhstan, where some five million Russians live and where the population is largely Russian.

Rising Russian nationalism, unfortunately, has been accompanied by emerging ethnic and racial violence. Newly found freedoms have enabled Russians to voice prejudices they had previously repressed. People from the Caucasus and Central Asia as well as others who do not appear to be Russian are often victims of abuse, harassment, and violence. The main victims have been Chechens, Azeris, Georgians, and Roma (Gypsies). Blacks may also be victims of verbal abuse and assaults on the streets.

Antisemitism, long latent in Russia (and at times not so latent), has also resurfaced. Jews have been subjected to harassment and violence, particularly in provinces where local leaders beyond Moscow's control resort to antisemitism for political purposes. The main perpetrators of ethnic violence today are skinheads, young men in their late teens who shave their heads and dress in combat gear. Some are affiliated with groups of football fans; others are linked to a neo-Nazi movement. All share a hatred of foreigners, among whom they include Jews and others whose families have lived in Russia for centuries.

Despite the exodus to Israel in the 1990s, there has been a renaissance of Jewish life for Russia's estimated one million Jews. The number of Jewish communities reached 140 in the year 2000, more than double the number two years earlier, and such communities are located in all parts of the country. People of Jewish descent are prominent in science, medicine, literature, and the arts as well as in politics and public life. Antisemitism, once state policy under the Soviets, has been disavowed by President Vladimir Putin.

Russians and other citizens of the former Soviet Union are very much aware of their nationality. Proud of their ethnicity, they are also curious about the national origins of persons they encounter. They will be pleased to tell foreign visitors about their own nationality, and visitors should not hesitate to ask.

Religion

A man who was not Orthodox could not be Russian.
—Fyodor Dostoyevsky, *The Possessed*

Russian ethnicity, culture, and nationalism have been identi-
fied with Russian Orthodoxy, the state religion of Russia for a
thousand years. In every ethnic Russian there is an Orthodox
heritage. It can emerge when least expected, even among convinced communists. Fyodor Dostoyevsky's dictum, however,
would be challenged today by many Russians who do not
profess Orthodoxy or any religion at all.

In a country that, under the communists, had supposedly been
almost completely atheist, slightly more than half of the people
today identify themselves as believers. Polls show that, during
the 1990s, 51 percent were followers of Russian Orthodoxy; some
2 percent, other branches of Christianity; 3 percent, Islam; 0.5
percent, Judaism; 0.5 percent, other religions; 34 percent, atheism; and 10 percent, agnosticism.[II]

Russian citizens with an Islamic heritage, although mostly
secular, number some twenty million and have become a growing
concern to the Moscow government. Muslims are a majority in
seven republics of the Russian Federation, and their birth rate is
higher than that of ethnic Russians. An estimated one million
Muslims live in Moscow. In Chechnya, rebels who began their
opposition with a focus on sovereignty or independence, now
identify with Muslim fundamentalism. And on Russia's southern flank, in the Caucasus and Central Asia, resurgent Islamic
extremism worries governments there as well as in Moscow.

Religious belief is related to age. In Russia, 67 percent of people
over pension age are believers, as are 47 to 48 percent of those
aged 18 to 35. Religious belief is also more widespread among
women, with 64 percent of women identifying themselves as
believers, compared with only 40 percent of men. Rural residents
are not significantly more religious than urban; religious belief
differs substantially, however, among regions, with 66 percent
identifying themselves as believers in the Trans-Volga heartland

---

[II] These statistics, and the following, are from "What Faith Will Save
Us?," *Novoye Vremya* (Moscow), 14 October 2001.

area of Russia, compared with only 44 percent in northwestern Russia, for example.

Despite their religious beliefs, Russians still reflect much of their pagan, pre-Christian past. A superstitious people, they just do not do certain things, and neither should visitors. Shaking hands across a threshold is believed to bring bad luck; in traditional Russian folklore, the doorway is where the house spirit is believed to reside. Whistling indoors brings poverty. Sit at the corner of a table and you will never marry. And when you make a new purchase, you must drink to it or it will be lost, stolen, or vandalized. Many of these beliefs reflect a fascination with the occult, which has been noted throughout Russian history and is now experiencing a revival.

Literature on astrology, palmistry, numerology, and the interpretation of dreams can be found everywhere in bookstores and sidewalk kiosks, and interest in such subjects is not limited to common people. Gorbachev's horoscope was published in a Moscow newspaper. Brezhnev was treated by a Georgian faith healer in his final years. Boris Yeltsin had a team of Kremlin astrologers whose sole job was to help him make decisions.

Sorcery and witchcraft also have many believers in Russia. Newspapers advertise the services of clairvoyants, witches, and sorcerers. A weekly Moscow TV show advises viewers on how sorcery and witchcraft can improve their daily lives. And in the *Duma* (parliament) elections of December 1999, astrologers were consulted by newspapers, businesspeople, and politicians, all seeking to predict the prospects of the various candidates. All this occurs in a country that has been Christian for more than a thousand years.

The origins of the Russian Church are in Byzantium, the Eastern branch of Christianity. Because of its Byzantine beginnings, the Russian Church regards itself as a direct descendant of the early Christian communities. From Byzantium also came the belief that Orthodox Christianity, as James Billington writes,

had solved all the basic problems of belief and worship. All that was needed was "right praising" (the literal translation of *pravoslaviye*, the Russian version of the Greek *orthodoxos*) through forms of worship handed down by the Apostolic Church and defined for all time by its seven ecumenical councils. Changes in dogma or even sacred phraseology could not be tolerated, for there was but one answer to any controversy. (1970, 6)

The consensus of the Orthodox congregation was regarded as the truth—a singularity of truth in which there was no room for a pluralism of opinion. In this idea lie the roots of Russia's traditional disdain for dissidents—political as well as religious. The Russian word for *dissident, inakomyslyaschi,* actually means "a person who thinks differently."

Also with roots in Russian Orthodoxy is the Russian sense of community and egalitarianism. *Sobor,* the Russian word for cathedral (as well as council), indicates a coming together of congregants who share common Christian values. Stites describes *sobor* as signifying a "sense of harmonious spiritual community" (1989, 16).

Sobor is a symbolic word for Russians, who regard Roman Catholicism as too authoritarian and Protestantism as too individualistic. Catholicism is seen as authoritarian because each Catholic believer and each national church must submit to the authority of the Pope. Protestantism is too individualistic because each national church can make its own religious doctrine and can be further splintered from within. In Orthodoxy, by contrast, as Paul Miliukov put it, "A national authority could never conflict with the universal doctrine of the Eastern church, because the national churches had no power to introduce changes into the universal doctrine, and the universal doctrine had not been invested with power" (1960, 134).

Thus, while churches in the West labored vigorously to achieve independence in religious matters, in the East the creation of national churches came easily because there was no need to question religious doctrine that, as Billington noted above, had been defined for all time and was universally accepted. Russia was the first nation to have a national Orthodox Church, but its example was followed by Greece, Georgia, Serbia, Romania, Bulgaria, and others. While autonomous, they are all members of the one Eastern Church.

Russian Orthodoxy is also seen as egalitarian, a fellowship uniting all souls under a single and correct religious rite. The Orthodox vision of sobornost is described by Zernov as "the main driving force behind all the social and political endeavors of the Russian...the expression of the desire to treat their rapidly expanding state as one big family" (1978, 182). Among Orthodox Christians there is indeed a feeling of family.

Easter, the principal Russian religious holiday, has a special meaning for Russians, who become euphoric as their long and harsh winter draws to an end. For them, Easter signifies the resurrection of nature, when after six months of the immobility and death of winter, life suddenly returns to the land. Historically, the end of two centuries of Mongol rule is seen as a resurrection of the Russian people, achieved through their Christian faith.

At Easter the Resurrection, for Russians, has its full meaning in Christ's victory over sin and death. "The service on Easter night," writes Zernov, "is an experience that has no parallel in the worship of other nations. Only those who have been present at this service can realize all that the Resurrection means to the Russian people" (179). Visitors who are in Russia in the spring should be sure to attend an Easter service.

Under the Soviets, atheism became official doctrine, and the Orthodox Church, with its tradition of submission to state authority—another legacy of Byzantium—proved vulnerable, easy to suppress and control. From a historical perspective, in old Russia there was one church, one truth, and little tolerance for dissidents. In the Soviet era—at least before 1985—the Communist Party replaced the Church, and party ideology supplanted religious truth, while intolerance of dissidents greatly increased and became state policy.

As a substitute church, the Communist Party established a cult of Lenin, the founder and father of the Soviet state, and his portraits and busts became the icons of the new religion. Every school, workplace, and many homes had a *krasny ugol* (literally, red corner) in which an image of Lenin replaced a religious icon. And when Lenin died in 1924, he was embalmed and interred in a granite tomb next to the Kremlin, where thousands of Russians still wait patiently in line for hours every day to see his mummified remains.

The spirit of Lenin, regarded by orthodox communists as immortal, was embodied in the popular slogan, "Lenin lived, Lenin lives, Lenin will live." And in 1969, to remind Muscovites of Lenin's immortality, an image of Lenin was projected at night by searchlight onto a large balloon in the skies above the Kremlin during the anniversary of the centennial of his birth. The significance of this event (Lenin's birth was during the Easter season) was not lost on Russians who address each other at Easter with the traditional Orthodox greeting, "Christ has risen." Today, Lenin no longer lives but he still stands, as a statue, in the central square of many Russian provincial cities. And his followers rule almost half of Russia's administrative regions and hold a third of the seats in the Russian Duma.

After 1985 the antireligious policies of the Stalin years were reversed. A law on freedom of conscience was passed in 1990, and Russians, responding to a rebirth of interest in Russian cultural traditions, are showing renewed interest in their Church.

Although only slightly more than half of Russians today are believers in Orthodoxy—and only a small proportion of those are regular churchgoers—the Church is nevertheless supported by many nonbelievers who regard it as a symbol of Russian culture and an object of national pride. To endorse the renewed role of Orthodoxy in Russian life and to confirm his cordial relationship with the Church, President Putin has admitted to being baptized as a child and openly asserts that he is a believer.

Russia in 2001 had 19,000 parishes, nearly triple the number existing in 1988, and more were being added despite the shortage of trained priests. Churches confiscated by the communists are being restored, and Moscow's imposing Cathedral of Christ the

Savior, the world's largest Orthodox church, has been rebuilt. It overlooks the Moscow River not far from the Kremlin. Religious institutions are also again free to do charitable work, and the Church has also branched into business activities such as banking, hotels, and light manufacturing. Orthodox Christmas—which falls on January 7 under the old Julian calendar—is once more a state holiday, as it was prior to 1918. Clearly, Orthodoxy is again a force in Russia, as attested by a poll taken in January 2000 that showed that the two most trusted institutions were the army and the Russian Church (Colton and McFaul 2001, 11). Moreover, Orthodoxy appears to be looking more and more like the state religion it once was, as robed priests give their blessings at major government and public events.

Foreign-based missionaries, many of them from Britain and the United States, are also now active in Russia despite efforts by the Orthodox Church to place restrictions on them. A law passed in 1997 threatens to jeopardize the status of the 17,000 non-Orthodox religious groups in Russia. The four religions regarded as traditional—Christianity, Islam, Judaism, and Buddhism—are exempt, however.

Under this law, groups not registered with the state—a difficult and time-consuming process—cannot own property or conduct public services. Likely to be affected by the law are certain Protestant, Catholic, and Muslim congregations as well as Scientologists, Jehovah's Witnesses, Hare Krishnas, and the Salvation Army. In September 2001, for example, a court shut down the Moscow chapter of the British-based Salvation Army, which runs soup kitchens for poor and elderly Muscovites. The city had charged that the Salvation Army had failed to register on time or prove the need for its continued existence as the law requires. Moreover, because its members wear uniforms, they have been accused by some of being part of a militarized force, intent on overthrowing the Russian government.

The United States, in contrast to Russia, has had neither a state church, an official ideology, nor a single truth. Rather, it has known a pluralism of beliefs and truths, and has tolerated, if not encouraged, dissenters from these truths. The country was settled initially by large numbers of religious and political dissidents from Europe who were more interested in worshiping God in their own way than in imposing their beliefs on others. Church and state have been kept separate, religion and ideology have been excluded from state affairs, and diverse views have been welcomed. Indeed, the very right to be different has been respected.

Americans have resisted universal systems of thought as well as ideologies that purport to have the answers to all questions and a grand plan for future action. If Americans do have an ideology, it is pragmatism—if it works, do it.

In Russia, however, creating a consensus, whether in religion or politics, has been seen as desirable and dissidents as somewhat strange—if not at times insane—for refusing to join in. According to Harvard's Edward Keenan, Russians have a tendency to embrace a philosophical system that is not theirs to begin with and, after time, to proclaim themselves the sole custodians of its true interpretation (1985).

3

Culture and Character

The Russian is a delightful person till he tucks in his shirt. As an oriental he is charming. It is only when he insists upon being treated as the most easterly of western peoples instead of the most westerly of easterns that he becomes a racial anomaly and extremely difficult to handle. The host never knows which side of his nature is going to turn up next.

—Rudyard Kipling, *The Man Who Was*

Egalitarianism

The interests of distribution and egalitarianism always predominated over those of production and creativity in the minds and emotions of the Russian intelligentsia.

—Nikolai Berdyaev, in *Vekhi*

Americans are raised on the success ethic—work hard, get ahead, be successful in whatever you do. The success ethic, however, is alien to many Russians, who believe that it may be morally wrong to get ahead, particularly at the expense of others. Russians will not mind if their American acquaintances are successful, but they are likely to resent fellow Russians who "succeed." Belief in communism has eroded, but the egalitarian ethic still survives.

"In Russia," writes Nina Khrushcheva,

> "equality of outcomes," a belief that material conditions in so-
> ciety should not vary too greatly among individuals and classes,
> wins out over Western "equality of opportunities," which tends
> to tolerate and even encourage the open flourishing of class dis-
> tinctions. Therefore, working for money, for example, a virtue so
> respected in the West, was not a "good way" in Russia. Russians
> can be great workers, as long as labor is done not for profit but
> for some spiritual or personal reason or is done as a heroic deed,
> performing wonders, knowing no limits. (2000/2001, 48)

Egalitarianism is a social philosophy that advocates the re-
moval of inequities among persons and a more equal distribution
of benefits. In its Russian form egalitarianism is not an invention
of communists but has its roots in the culture of the mir, which,
as we have seen, represented village democracy, Russian-style.

The mir's governing body was an assembly composed of heads
of households, including widowed women, and presided over
by a *starosta* (elder). Before the introduction of currency, mir
members were economically equal, and equality for members
was considered more important than personal freedom. Those
agricultural communes, with their egalitarian lifestyle and distribution of material benefits, were seen by Russian intellectuals as necessary to protect the simple peasants from the harsh
competition of Western individualism. Individual rights, it was
feared, would enable the strong to prosper but cause the weak
to suffer. Others saw the mir as a form of agrarian socialism, the
answer to Russia's striving for egalitarianism.

For much of Russian history, peasants numbered close to 90 percent of the population. By 1990, however, the figure had dropped
to near 30 percent due to industrialization. But although the other
70 percent of the population lives in urban areas, most of today's
city dwellers are only one, two, or three generations removed
from their ancestral villages. The peasant past is still very much
with them, and despite their urbanization and education, many
of them still think in the egalitarian terms of the mir.

The Soviet state also thought in egalitarian terms. Communism aimed to make a complete break with the past and create a new society, but its leaders could not escape the heritage of the past, and their leveling of society revived the communal ethic of the mir on a national scale. As British scholar Geoffrey Hosking observed, "In some ways...the Soviet state has perpetuated the attitudes of the pre-1930 Russian village community. The expectation is still prevalent that the community will guarantee essentials in a context of comradely indigence just above the poverty line" (1990, 132).

Many aspects of Russian communism may indeed be traced to the mir. The meetings of the village assembly were lively, but decisions were usually unanimous and binding on all members. This provided a precedent for the "democratic centralism" of communism under which issues were debated, decisions were made that all Party members were obliged to support, and opposition was prohibited.

Peasants could not leave the mir without an internal passport, issued only with permission of their household head. This requirement was a precursor not only of Soviet (and tsarist) regulations denying citizens freedom of movement and resettlement within the country but also of the practice of denying emigration to those who did not have parental permission. Under communism, the tapping of telephones and the perusal of private mail by the Committee on State Security (KGB) must have seemed natural to leaders whose ancestors lived in a mir, where the community was privy to the personal affairs of its members. And in a society where the bulk of the population was tied to the land and restricted in movement, defections by Soviet citizens abroad were seen as treasonous.

Despite its egalitarian ethic, old Russia also had an entrepreneurial tradition based in a small merchant class called *kupyechestvo*. Russian merchants established medieval trading centers, such as the city-state of Novgorod, which were independent and self-governing until absorbed by Muscovy in the late fifteenth century. Merchants explored and developed Siberia and played a key role in Russia's industrialization of the late nineteenth and early twentieth centuries.

Merchants were also Westernizers in the years between the revolutions of 1905 and 1917, endorsing social and legal reform, the rule of law, civil liberties, and broader educational opportunities. They rejected economic liberalism with its emphasis on free trade in international exchange and free competition in the domestic economy, however, advocating instead state planning. And as an additional link in the chain of continuity between the old and new Russia, as Ruth Roosa has pointed out, merchants in the years prior to 1917 called for state plans of five, ten, and even fifteen years' duration embracing all aspects of economic life (1963, 198–218).

Agriculture in old Russia also had its entrepreneurs. Most of the land was held in large estates by the crown, aristocracy, and landed gentry, but after the emancipation of the serfs in 1861, a small class of independent farmers emerged. By 1917, on the eve of the Revolution, some 10 percent of the peasants were independent farmers. The more enterprising and prosperous among them were called *kulaks* (fists) by their less successful and envious brethren who had remained in the mir. But the kulaks were ruthlessly exterminated and their land forcibly collectivized by the communists in the early 1930s. Millions of peasants left the land they had farmed, production was disrupted, and more than five million died in the resulting famine. The forced collectivization contributed to the eventual failure of Soviet agriculture.

Private farming returned to Russia in the late 1980s and grew steadily over the next few years, encouraged by former President Mikhail Gorbachev's perestroika, legislation passed by the Russian Parliament, and decrees issued by Boris Yeltsin. The legal underpinning for agricultural reform was provided by Article 36 of the new Russian Constitution, approved by the electorate in December 1993, which affirmed that "Citizens and their associations shall be entitled to have land in private ownership." Parliament, however, reflecting historic attitudes on communal ownership of land, balked at passing legislation that would have put that article into effect (Belyakov and Raymond 1994, 27). The opposition in parliament was led by the Communist and

Agrarian Parties, and most land remained government property, as it was during Soviet times when communist ideology required that the state own the means of production.

That changed on October 26, 2001, when President Vladimir Putin, bringing to a close a decade of efforts by Russia's leadership to ease Soviet-era land sale restrictions, put his pen to legislation giving Russians the right to purchase land for industrial purposes and urban housing, the two most profitable sectors of the Russian land market. Then, on June 26, 2002, the lower house of Parliament approved legislation that would allow the sale of Russian farmland for the first time since the 1917 Bolshevik Revolution but added an amendment that permits foreigners to lease agricultural land but not purchase it.

Opponents of farmland sales, in addition to their ideological misgivings, believe that such sales will open the way for wealthy Russians and foreign investors to buy up or lease large tracts of land.

Supporters of farmland sales believe they will further Russia's transition to a market economy, encourage foreign investment, improve agricultural productivity, promote growth of a property-owning class, provide revenue by taxing privately owned land, and curb the corruption that has facilitated illegal land transactions.

Despite all the supportive legislation and decrees, private agriculture is still not widely accepted by Russian peasants, most of whom oppose reform and are reluctant to leave the security of the former collective and state farms for the risks of the free market.* Impediments to private farming include difficulties in acquiring enough land and equipment to start a farm, a general lack of credit, the reluctance of peasants to give up the broad range of social services provided by the collective and state farms,

---

* Much of the data on agriculture here has been drawn from Roy L. Prosterman, et al., "Russian Agrarian Reform: A Status Report from the Field" (Seattle: Rural Development Institute, August 1994).

and a fear that if land reform is reversed they will once more be branded as kulaks and will lose their land.

By the year 2000, there were some 290,000 private farms in Russia, accounting for 6 percent of the country's farmland but providing only 2 percent of agricultural output because at least half those farms were not operating (www.ers.usda.gov/briefing/ Russia/polycies.htm). The formation of new private farms has slowed, and Russian agriculture is still dominated by what were formerly large state and collective farms. Moreover, those farms that had been privatized as joint stock companies were still being run as before, by the same managers, and with the same results. A comparison of agriculture in Russia and North America shows that, for the same amount of land, material input, and labor, Russian farms produce less than half as much as U.S. and Canadian farms in similar climatic areas. Yet with all its failures, collectivized agriculture is still the principal source of food for the Russian people and will likely continue to be so for some time.

Economic reforms have also been slow to gain support among the general public, particularly the older generation. While there is a streak of individualism in many Russians, the entrepreneurial spirit of the businessperson and independent farmer runs counter to Russian egalitarianism. For many Russians, selling goods for profit is regarded as dishonest and is called *spekulatsiya* (speculation). Russians, it has been said, would rather bring other people down to their level than try to rise higher, a mentality known as *uravnilovka* (leveling).

Caution and Conservatism

The slower you go, the further you'll get.

—Russian proverb

Living in a country that claimed to be socialist, Russians were assumed by many in the West to be radicals and challengers of the established order. In reality, they are more likely to be cautious and conservative defenders of the status quo, and with good reason. Their cruel climate, harsh history, and skeptical outlook on life have caused Russians to value stability, security, social order, and predictability and to avoid risk. Major changes are feared, and the tried and tested is preferred over the new and unknown.

Caution and conservatism are also legacies of the peasant past. Barely eking out a living in small isolated villages, peasants had to contend not only with the vagaries of nature but also with the strictures of communal life, authoritarian fathers, all-powerful officials, and reproachful religious leaders. In a traditional agricultural society, stability was valued, and change came slowly. As Marshall Shulman of Columbia University has put it, "Russians feel obliged to defend their traditional values against the onslaught of the modern world" (1989).

The experience of the twentieth century has given Russians no cause to discard their caution. "Man-made catastrophes," writes Stephen F. Cohen of New York University, "have repeatedly victimized millions of ordinary [Russian] citizens and officials alike—the first European war, revolution, civil war, two great famines, forced collectivization, Stalin's terror, World War II, and more." From these events, concludes Cohen, has come a conservatism which is "a real bond between state and society—and thus the main obstacle to change" (1985, 148).

Caution and conservatism can also be seen at the highest levels of government, where most of the leadership has been of peasant origin. Reflecting their peasant past, Russia's leaders will take advantage of every opportunity to advance their cause but will be careful to avoid undue risk.

The cautious approach was recommended by Gorbachev in a talk in Washington during his June 1990 summit with President George H. W. Bush. Noting that he preferred not to act precipitously in resolving international differences, Gorbachev advocated an approach that "is more humane. That is, to be very cautious, to consider a matter seven times, or even one hundred times before one makes a decision" (*The New York*

Times, 1 June 1990). Yeltsin was also overly cautious when it was in his interest and Russia's to be bold and daring. In June 1991, when he enjoyed high prestige and popularity after his election as president, and in August of that year after he foiled an attempted coup, Yeltsin's caution prevented him from instituting the broad reforms that Russia required. Some speak of a congenital Russian inertia. As an old Russian proverb puts it, "The Russian won't budge until the roasted rooster pecks him in the rear."

Americans will have their patience tested by Russian caution. A nation of risk takers, most Americans are descendants of immigrants who dared to leave the known of the Old World for the unknown of the New. In the United States risk takers have had the opportunity to succeed or to fail in the attempt. Indeed, risk is the quintessence of a market economy. The opportunities of the New World, with its social mobility and its stability, have helped Americans to accentuate the positive. For Russians, geography and history have caused them to anticipate the negative.

Pessimism

> We did the best we could, but it turned out as usual.
> —Viktor Chernomyrdin, former Russian Prime Minister

Russian pessimism is the source of many anekdots. According to one, pessimists say, "Things can't be worse than they are now." Optimists say, "Yes they can." Another anekdot describes a Russian pessimist as a realistic optimist. Foreign business representatives will have to become realistic optimists themselves in appraising prospects for their ventures in Russia.

Russian pessimism contrasts with American innocence and optimism. Americans expect things to go well and become annoyed when they do not. Russians expect things to go poorly and have learned to live with misfortune.

Americans, for example, like happy endings in their horoscopes as well as in their novels and films. Russian astrologers and writers spin tales of tragedy. American horoscopes are generally upbeat, with such advice as "Everything seems to be going your way. You are very original; there is no one else like you. Your finances will be better than anticipated." Russian horoscopes, by contrast, are full of gloom and doom, advising, "This month will bring the loss of friends and protectors, hostility, and deceit. All attempts to interfere with the natural course of events and to change it for the better will lead to no good results. You should not expect anything good from your family life today. Don't be frantic when you learn that all your savings are gone."

However, the pessimism of astrologers apparently does not apply to their horoscopes for the nation. In a 2001 end-of-the-year press conference, Russia's most prominent astrologist, Pavel Globa, predicted that the year 2002 would be very successful for Russia. Political and economic developments would be positive, he said, reforms would continue, there will be no crises, and after crucial changes in the coming year, Russia would again be a superpower (*RIA Novosti*, 21 December 2001). Readers of these pages will be able to see if his predictions hold true.

Putting astrologers' predictions aside, life has indeed been difficult for Russians. Weather, wars, violence, cataclysmic changes, and oppressive rule have made pessimists of them. Russians have a "gloom-and-doom mentality," writes translator Richard Lourie. "Both at the kitchen table and in print, they indulge in apocalyptic prophecies" (1991, 82).

When asked to explain the grounds for his pessimism, a Russian professor told me: "Our main concern, that which determines all our actions and feelings, is *strakh* (fear). The world is dangerous, and we must be careful."

Strakh will be encountered in many places but particularly among liberals and intellectuals whose hopes for reforms and a better future have been shattered several times, first by Nikita Khrushchev, then by Gorbachev, and more recently by Yeltsin. Americans should not be put off by this gloom and doom, nor should they attempt to make optimists of Russians. The best response is to express understanding and sympathy.

44

When asked how things are, a Russian is likely to reply *normalno* (normal), which might be translated as "not too bad." Translators Richard Lourie and Aleksei Mikhalev go further, describing *normalno* as "a wistful, ironic word, containing all the pain that came before and all of the hope of what might yet come to pass, the great dream of the present, 'a normal' society" (1989, 38).

Less in control of their lives than Americans and other Europeans, Russians feel caught up in the big sweeps of history where the individual is insignificant and does not count. As Lourie and Mikhalev explain, the difference is simple and dramatic:

> For us, history is a subject, a black-and-white newsreel; for them it is a tank on their street, a search of their apartment by strangers with power.... Nearly every life has been touched directly, branded, by the great historical spasms of revolution, war and terror. For a Russian, repression always comes from the outside world.... (38)

Glasnost and perestroika were exciting for foreigners to observe from a distance. But to Russians, they were yet another historical spasm with attendant uncertainties about the future. Today, many Russians see their country threatened by ethnic warfare and environmental degradation. Some Russians even speak of genetic degradation.

The best and brightest have traditionally been banished. In old Russia independent thinkers were exiled to Siberia. Following the Bolshevik Revolution, the cream of Russia's elite was liquidated. Joseph Stalin's purges of the 1930s further decimated the intelligentsia, and today many of Russia's best and brightest are being lost through emigration.

One of those who emigrated is Vladimir Voinovich, a popular and critically acclaimed writer and human rights advocate who was forced to leave for the West in 1975 after the KGB suggested to him that his future in the Soviet Union would be "unbearable." A satirist in the tradition of Gogol, Nikolai Voinovich has described how Americans and Russians react differently to his writing. "Russians and Americans," he writes, "read my books in very different ways. Americans usually say they are funny. Russians say...they are very gloomy, dark" (*The New York Times*, 28 November 1989). This gloomy and dark side of the Russian character explains the bittersweet humor that is native to Russia and the "good news, bad news" jokes. (Voinovich later returned to Russia and now divides his time between Moscow, Munich, and New York.)

Russian pessimism can also be infectious, and Americans who have worked with them for many years are vulnerable to the virus. Llewellyn Thompson, twice American ambassador to Moscow, was asked on his retirement in 1968 to name his greatest accomplishment. "That I didn't make things any worse," replied the veteran diplomat.[†]

Despite their pessimism and complaining, there is an admirable durability about Russians, a hardy people who have more than proven their ability to endure severe deprivation and suffer lengthy hardships. Tibor Szamuely has written of "the astonishing durability of...certain key social and political institutions, traditions, habits, and attitudes, their staying power, their essential stability amidst the turbulent currents of violent change, chaotic upheaval, and sudden innovation" (1974, 6).

One might ask what has sustained Russia for more than a thousand years. "The strength of the people," explains maestro Mstislav Rostropovich, "is the strength of Russia" (1990).

Extremes and Contradictions

Contradiction is...the essence of Russia. West and East, Pacific and Atlantic, Arctic and tropics, extreme cold and extreme heat, prolonged sloth and sudden feats of energy, exaggerated cruelty

---

[†] In his final briefing for American correspondents prior to his departure from Moscow in 1968, a meeting the author attended.

and exaggerated kindness, ostentatious wealth and dismal squa-
lor, violent xenophobia and uncontrollable yearning for contact
with the foreign world, vast power and the most abject slavery,
simultaneous love and hate for the same objects.... The Russian
does not reject these contradictions. He has learned to live with
them, and in them. To him, they are the spice of life.

—George F. Kennan, *Memoirs*

President Harry Truman once quipped that he was looking for
a one-armed economist because all his economic advisers concluded their advice by saying, "but, on the other hand." Americans, with their proclivity for rational consistency, seek clear and
precise responses, but they usually end up by falling back to a
middle position that avoids contradictions and extremes.

Russians, by contrast, have a well-deserved reputation for
extremes. When emotions are displayed, they are spontaneous
and strong. Russian hospitality can be overwhelming, friendship
all encompassing, compassion deep, loyalty long lasting, drinking
heavy, celebrations boisterous, obsession with security paranoid,
and violence vicious. With Russians, it is often all or nothing.
Halfway measures simply do not suffice.

"The Anglo-Saxon instinct," writes George F. Kennan, distinguished U.S. diplomat and historian, "is to attempt to smooth
away contradictions, to reconcile opposing elements, to achieve
something in the nature of an acceptable middle ground as a
basis for life." The Russian, continues Kennan, tends to deal only
in extremes, "and he is not particularly concerned to reconcile
them" (1967, 528). The American mind, concludes Kennan,
will not understand Russia until it accepts that

> because a proposition is true, the opposite of that proposition is
> not false. It must agree never to entertain a proposition about
> the Russian world without seeking, and placing in apposition to
> it, its inevitable and indispensable opposite. Then it must agree
> to regard both as legitimate, valid conceptions...to understand
> that Russian life at any given moment is not the common ex-
> pression of harmonious integrated elements, but a precarious and

evershifting equilibrium between numbers of conflicting forces.... Right and wrong, reality and unreality, are determined in Russia, not by any God, not by any innate nature of things, but simply by men themselves. Here men determine what is true and what is false. (529)

Russian extremes and contradictions have also been described by poet Yevgeny Yevtushenko: "I am thus and not thus, I am industrious and lazy, determined and shiftless. I am...shy and impudent, wicked and good; in me is a mixture of everything from the west to the east, from enthusiasm to envy..." (in Mehnert 1961, 30).

Human feelings count for much in Russia, and those who do not share the depth of those feelings will be considered cold and distant. When Russians open their souls to someone, it is a sign of acceptance and sharing. Westerners will have to learn to drop their stiff upper lips and also to open their souls.

The Russian Soul

The famous "Russian soul" was to no small extent the product of this agonizing uncertainty regarding Russia's proper geographical, social, and spiritual position in the world, the awareness of a national personality that was split between East and West.
—Tibor Szamuely, *The Russian Tradition*

Andrei Amalryk, the political dissident I used to visit in the small room he shared with his wife in a Moscow communal apartment, was in trouble with the Soviet authorities for most of his adult life. During his sentence to political exile in faraway Magadan, just across the Bering Strait from Alaska, Amalryk encountered by chance the man who had denounced him to the authorities. The denouncer expressed regret, asked forgiveness, and suggested they have a drink. After consuming a bottle of vodka—which got both of them drunk—the denouncer became even more remorseful and asked Amalryk what he could do to make amends. Amalryk suggested that he write an account of

48

what he had done. The denouncer wrote out a confession of how he had succumbed to KGB pressure to falsify his testimony, signed it, and presented it to Amalryk with deep emotion. A few hours later, however, sober and no longer remorseful, he asked that it be returned to him and, when Amalryk refused, even offered to buy it back (1982, 271).

Russkaya dusha (Russian soul) can turn up suddenly in the most unexpected places, and just as suddenly disappear. Just when foreigners believe that Russians are about to get down to serious business, they can become decidedly emotional and unbusiness-like. Dusha is well known in the arts, where it manifests itself as emotion, sentimentality, exuberance, energy, theatricality, flamboyant virtuosity, and bravura technique. Dusha, however, transcends the arts and is the essence of Russian behavior.

A romantic ethos, dusha appeals to feeling rather than fact, sentiment over certainty, suffering instead of satisfaction, and nostalgia for the past as opposed to the reality of the present. In a broader sense, dusha is also a reaffirmation of the purity of traditional Russian values against the encroachment of Western enlightenment, rationalism, and secularism, especially in things cultural.

Russian dusha is often derided in the West as a fantasy of artists, composers, and writers. If dusha ever really existed, this argument goes, it was the product of a traditional agricultural society which had very little in material goods to offer. In a modern industrial society, the argument continues, dusha is quickly forgotten and Russians become as realistic, practical, materialistic, and unromantic as Westerners.

The truth lies somewhere in between. Russians do have a rich spirituality that does indeed contrast with Western rationalism, materialism, and pragmatism. Russians suffer but seem to enjoy their suffering. Obsessed with ideas, their conversation is weighty and lengthy. The rational and pragmatic approach does not always work for them. More often, it is personal relations, feelings, and traditional values that determine a course of action.

Westerners are more likely to depend on the cold facts and to do what works.

As Tatyana Tolstaya, one of Russia's leading contemporary writers, says,

> Logical categories are inapplicable to the soul. But Russian sensitivity, permeating the whole culture, doesn't want to use logic—logic is seen as dry and evil, logic comes from the devil—the most important thing is sensation, smell, emotion, tears, mist, dreams, and enigma. (1990, 4)

"In Russian culture, emotion is assigned an entirely positive value," writes Tolstaya; "the more a person expresses his emotions, the better, more sincere, and more 'open' he is" (4). The Russian mentality, she believes, has penetrated to some degree all corners of the country, "often not for the best." Dusha is described by Tolstaya as

> sensitivity, reverie, imagination, an inclination to tears, compassion, submission mingled with stubbornness, patience that permits survival in what would seem to be unbearable circumstances, poetry, mysticism, fatalism, a penchant for walking the dark, humid back streets of consciousness, introspection, sudden, unmotivated cruelty, mistrust of rational thought, fascination with the word—the list could go on and on—all these qualities that have frequently been attributed to the "Slavic soul." (4)

But that Slavic soul also has many aspects that Westerners can respect and admire. As Northwestern University professor Irwin Weil puts it,

> Russians maintain their integrity in a way that conforms to their inner notion of what a human being should be, in a manner they consider proper, and with an honesty and decency that I have seldom seen anywhere else in the world. Above all, they have an appreciation for *tselnost* (wholeness, complete commitment) and faith, no matter what that faith may be related to. To be

a real human being, one must maintain that full commitment and respect it in other people as well. In this sense, it makes no difference to them whether the other person is a Marxist or a reactionary. (1991)

Russians are sensitive to the feelings of others as well as their own. Weil recalls how, during the Cuban missile crisis of 1962, Cuban students at Moscow State University placed signs calling President John F. Kennedy an s.o.b. above the doors to their dormitory rooms. Russian students complained to the student council that the signs were offensive to American students at the university, and the student council ordered that they be removed. On the death of President Kennedy in 1963, Weil received three letters from Russian friends expressing their personal condolences. And in 2001, after the World Trade Center disaster in New York, we received similar messages of condolence from Russian friends and acquaintances.

Other examples of Russian soul are the courage and moral strength of the Soviet Union's two most prominent political dissidents, Andrei Sakharov and Aleksandr Solzhenitsyn, in the face of KGB harassment and persecution. Their politics differed—Sakharov was a Westernizer, and Solzhenitsyn is a Slavophile—but both were awarded Nobel Prizes, the former for peace, the latter for literature.

Sakharov, the celebrated nuclear physicist who helped to develop the Soviet hydrogen bomb, suffered seven years of internal exile in Gorky (now Nizhny Novgorod) for his outspoken opposition to the Soviet war in Afghanistan. Returning to Moscow in 1986, ailing but unbroken in spirit, a year after Gorbachev's coming to power, he continued his struggle for human rights and led the democratic opposition until his untimely death in 1989.

Solzhenitsyn, after a search of his house by the KGB in 1971, during which one of his friends was brutally beaten, had the courage to send an indignant open letter of protest to Yuri Andropov, head of the KGB at the time. In his letter, Solzhenitsyn demanded from Andropov "the public identification of all the intruders, their punishment as criminals, and a public explanation of this incident. Otherwise I can only conclude that they were sent by *you*" (1975, 497–98). Solzhenitsyn, author of *The Gulag Archipelago*, an exposé of Stalin's slave labor camps, survived his challenge to the KGB but was exiled from the Soviet Union in 1974. After twenty years of exile in Vermont, he returned to Russia in 1994.

In the early years of the twenty-first century, the Russian soul is still spirited. Old virtues endure—respect for parents, deference to old age, regard for learning. Belief in village virtues is still strong—self-sacrifice, sense of duty, compassion, importance of family, love of nature. These aspects of the Russian soul are again the themes of "village writers," as they are known, who glorify peasant life and encourage a renaissance of traditional Russian values. Students hang on the words of their professors. Grateful audiences present flowers to musical and theatrical performers. Before vacating a home where they have lived for some time, Russians will sit quietly for a minute or two, reflecting on the events they have experienced there. Even in the postindustrial age, Russians demonstrate that emotions and personal feelings still matter.

But today, fear for the future of the Russian soul bothers Russians. Their dusha has survived centuries of church and state domination and seventy years of communism. Will it also survive, they wonder, the transition to the free market and democracy, and the call of American culture?

Big Is Beautiful

In its grandiose schemes, which were always on a worldwide scale, communism makes use of the Russian disposition for making plans and castle-building, which had hitherto no scope for practical application.
—Nikolai Berdyaev, *The Origin of Russian Communism*

"Sire, every thing is done on a large scale in this country—every thing is colossal" (1989, 183). So spoke the Marquis de Custine, addressing Tsar Nicholas in St. Petersburg in 1839 at the start of his travels through Russia. The French aristocrat was moved by the grand scale of "this colossal empire," as he described it in his four-volume *Russia in 1839*.

Modern-day travelers to Russia will also encounter colossal sights. In Moscow's Kremlin, guides point with pride to the Tsar Cannon—cast in 1586, with a bore of 36 inches and weight of 44 tons. Nearby is the Tsar Bell—20 feet high and, at 200 tons, the heaviest in the world.

Soviet leaders continued that "colossalism." When they industrialized, centralizing production to achieve economies of scale, they built gigantic industrial complexes employing up to 100,000 workers. *Gigantomania* is the term used by Western economists to describe that phenomenon. The Palace of Soviets, a Stalin project of the 1930s, was to have been the tallest building in the world, dwarfing the Empire State Building and the Eiffel Tower, and be topped by a 230-foot statue of Lenin. The Kremlin's Palace of Congresses, the huge hall known to Western TV viewers as the site of mass meetings, seats 6,000 and is one of the world's largest conference halls. Its snack bar can feed 3,000 people in ten minutes, thanks to the many Russian grandmothers who staff its bufet.

In Volgograd (formerly Stalingrad), the site of a decisive battle with Germany in World War II, a victorious Mother Russia, the largest full-figure statue in the world, towers 282 feet over the battlefield. And Russia's new victory monument to World War II, completed in 1995, is 465 feet high and topped by a 27-ton Nike, the goddess of victory.

Aeroflot was by far the world's largest airline, flying abroad as well as to the far corners of the Soviet Union. Its supersonic transport (SST), the world's first, was considerably larger than the Anglo-French Concorde. And when McDonald's opened its first hamburger restaurant in Moscow in 1990—on Pushkin Square, only a few blocks from the Kremlin—it was the largest McDonald's in the world, with a capacity of 900; it broke McDonald's worldwide opening day records for customers served. By 2001, the Pushkin Square McDonald's was still the busiest in the world, and McDonald's seventy-one restaurants in twenty-two Russian cities were serving 200,000 customers a day. That's a lot of *gamburgers*, as the Russians call them, since the German/English *h* is traditionally rendered in Russian as *g*.

Russians are impressed with size and numbers, and much that they do is on a grandiose scale. That is not unusual for a vast country. Russians think and act big, and they do not do things in a halfhearted way. Nor are these traits uniquely Russian. Americans, accustomed to wide open spaces, and with an expansive outlook on life, are also known to think big.

Big also describes the Russian military. Even after large reductions, Russia in 2002 had nearly 1.3 million people under arms. It also had the biggest missiles, submarines, and aircraft, and their numerical superiority over most U.S. equivalents has been used by the Pentagon in the past to justify requests for larger military budgets.[‡]

To be sure, the United States has to consider foreign capabilities in determining the forces needed to counter them. But when motives were sought for Russian advantages in conventional forces, all possibilities should have been considered. Did they need such large forces to defend their vast territory and long borders? Did they seek quantitative superiority to counter a U.S. qualitative lead? Did they build big because they did not have the technology to build small? Those were possible explanations that should have been considered in analyzing Russian motives. Another explanation, however, is simply that Russians are impressed with size and numbers. For Russians, big is beautiful.

Russia's grandiose plans have at times been realized and at other times, not. The Tsar Bell was too heavy and was neither

---

[‡] President Putin's plan to reform the military includes cutting manpower by one third, modernizing weapons, abolishing the draft, and making the military a fully professional force.

hung nor rung. The Tsar Cannon was too big to fire. The Palace of Soviets was abandoned after the foundation proved incapable of supporting the huge structure, and the site was used for an outdoor swimming pool—one of the largest in Europe, of course. The Soviet SST had major design problems and was shelved after several crashes, including one at the prestigious Paris Air Show. Aeroflot's extensive domestic network was broken up into nearly four hundred separate companies, with a drastic decline in safety standards. Russia's huge industrial plants have proven to be highly inefficient and noncompetitive, and the large state subsidies they require to avoid bankruptcy are an obstacle to their privatization. The Russian army's combat capabilities, as confirmed in the Chechnya war, have dramatically declined. And the *Kursk*, pride of the Russian navy and one of the largest submarines ever built, suffered an unexplained explosion in August 2000 and sank to the bottom of the Barents Sea with the loss of its entire crew of 118.

Russians, however, still have grand designs. In January 2001, Russian engineers unveiled their plan for a rail tunnel under the Bering Sea, linking Siberia and Alaska. There is also a plan to link St. Petersburg to Helsinki with a series of causeways and suspension bridges (*The Times* [London], 6 January 2001).

And what should be said of Moscow's current politics, the most recent of many attempts to reform Russia? The objective this time is to modernize, to make the nation more competitive with the West, and to regain its superpower status.

Will the sweeping reforms succeed, or are they merely the latest example of Russians thinking too big? History tells us to believe the latter. As Anton Chekhov put it one hundred years ago, "A Russian is particularly given to exalted ideas, but why is it he always falls so short in life? Why?"

Women—The Stronger Sex

Oh, Russian women, draft horses of the nation!
—Andrei Sinyavsky, *Goodnight!*

Some nations are called a fatherland, others a motherland. Russia is clearly a motherland. *Rodina*, "homeland," is feminine, and Mother Russia is the symbol of the nation. In this motherland, women are strong, hardworking, nurturing, long-suffering, and the true heroes of Russia. They hold the country together.

Russian literature, writes British scholar Ronald Hingley, again and again gives us situations

> in which a beautiful, strong, well-integrated, decisive young woman becomes erotically implicated with some spineless, dithering pipsqueak of a man who invariably emerges discredited from the involvement. In fiction of the totalitarian [Soviet] period the clash between strong female and weak male is more than ever in vogue, and has been well analyzed in terms which appropriately recall the life-cycle of the spider. (1977, 189)

The Bolsheviks professed to liberate women and give them full equality with men, and in the 1920s Soviet women enjoyed an equality under law unequaled anywhere else in the world. On this point Soviet law was explicit. As Article 35 of the 1977 Constitution declared,

> Women and men have equal rights in the USSR...ensured by according women equal access with men to education and vocational and professional training, equal opportunities in employment, remuneration and promotion, and in social and political and cultural activity. (38)

In practice, however, women were recognized but unrewarded. A state that claimed to have given all power to the people did in fact give power to only a few, and almost all of them were men.

During the entire Soviet era, only three women were named to the ruling Politburo of the Communist Party and almost none to high positions in the military and diplomatic corps. To be sure, the first woman ambassador of any country was an early Bolshevik, Aleksandra Kollontai, who was named Soviet Minister to Norway in 1923—but only after her ardent feminism and advocacy of free love put her on a collision course with Party leaders at home.

Women worked in factories and on farms to help build the Soviet economy, and they fought in World War II. The Soviet air force had three air groups "manned" entirely by women, flying bombers by night, dive bombers by day, and even fighter planes. Together, they flew more than 30,000 combat missions during World War II. One woman pilot, Lilya Litvak, had twelve "kills," making her an ace before she was shot down and died at age twenty-two.

In the new Russia, equal rights for women and men have been reaffirmed by Article 19 of the Constitution of 1993, which asserts, "The state shall guarantee equal human and civil rights and freedoms without regard to sex.... Men and women shall have equal rights and freedoms and equal opportunities to exercise them" (Belyakov and Raymond 1994, 22).

Women today are active in all professions and occupations but are especially strong in medicine where, reflecting an old Russian tradition, three-fourths of all doctors are women. They also predominate in teaching and in the textile, food, and social service industries. Women, however, are rarely seen in high government posts and seldom occupy supervisory or management posts. Full gender equality in the workforce is found only in the lowest-paying jobs, where women work as members of construction crews, farm laborers, street sweepers, and snow shovelers. But while few women occupy high government positions, in recent years they have been active in establishing a broad range of public and political organizations in the new civil society of Russia. Women are also becoming more active in business, founding and directing their own firms. Unfortunately, unemployment is much higher for women than for men, and many of them look for marriage abroad. Others turn to prostitution; literally thousands of streetwalkers can be seen in Moscow at night. Others are lured to the West by promises of employment but then find themselves prisoners in foreign bordellos.

Women actually work two shifts—one at the workplace and the other at home, where they put in another full workweek performing the duties of wife, mother, and homemaker. Moreover, as living standards have fallen, men have had to work longer hours and now do an even smaller share of the household tasks than before.

Sexual harassment in the workplace is common, as is wife beating at home. Thousands of women die each year from injuries suffered in domestic violence. Police generally take a hands-off attitude, and women do not know their rights in a country that still seems to believe a popular Russian adage, "If he beats you, it means that he loves you."

In his book *Perestroika*, Gorbachev said it was imperative to promote women to administrative posts and to involve them more actively in the management of the economy, cultural development, and public life. However, when discussing problems caused by weakened family ties, Gorbachev noted that heated debates are being held "about the question of what we should do to make it possible for women to return to their purely womanly mission" (1987, 116–17).

That "purely womanly mission" has been frustrated by recent history. Forty million Soviet men died in the three cataclysmic events of the Soviet era—the collectivization of agriculture, the political purges, and World War II—creating a severe shortage of men for two generations of women. Moreover, the mortality rate for men today is four times that of women in all age groups over twenty, largely because of alcoholism and related accidents and illnesses, and women outlive men, on average, by thirteen years. That explains why there are so many *babushki* (grandmothers) in Russia and so few *dyedushki* (grandfathers).

Attitudes on birth control stem from traditional Russian conservatism as well as from the views of a male-dominated leadership, which has sought to stabilize the family and increase the birthrate. Most families, however, avoid having a second child, due to limited housing (especially in the cities), the decline in state-subsidized day care, the collapse of the state welfare system, and the deterioration of health care as well as the increased cost of living. The use of contraceptives, now more available, has been rising slowly, but they are still not widely used, and family planning information is not readily available.

Abortion, legal and free in Russia since 1920, is still the common form of birth control, as it was in the Soviet Union. According to the Ministry of Health, 1.3 million pregnancies are annually registered in Russia, but 60 percent of women have abortions, 10 percent lose their unborn babies, and only 30 percent give live births. In addition, half of the women deciding to have their babies are anemic, and in 2001, nearly 59 percent of all newborns had various congenital diseases. Moreover 25 percent of deaths of women during pregnancy are caused by abortions, and earlier abortions affect following births and the health of future children. Not only women have serious reproductive problems. Some 69 percent of men under 50 in Russia also have them (*Johnson's Russia List*, #6499, 18 October 2002).

A few more facts will help to describe the status of women in Russia. One of every two marriages ends in divorce, and the number of single mothers and single women continues to rise. Nearly one-third of all babies born in Russia in the year 2000 were born to unwed mothers, double the percentage of a decade earlier, and 40 percent of those babies were born to teenagers (*Moscow Times*, 29 November 2001). Promiscuity is common but exists side by side with extreme modesty. While glasnost lowered official barriers to nudity and sexually explicit scenes in films, television, and theater, most Russians of the middle and older generations feel uncomfortable with those new liberties, and sex is not a subject for public discussion. Prudery also prevails. A woman will never ask a man for directions to the rest room; the man would be even more embarrassed than the woman.

Feminism, like many other movements originating in the West, has been late in reaching Russia. Grassroots women's groups are springing up around the country, but feminism is not yet a mass movement. The equality that Russian women want differs from that desired by Western women. Russian women see themselves as far more traditional in their dealings with men and in their views on domestic life. In dress and style, for example, they prefer glamor to comfort, femininity to practicality.

"The absence of a strong feminist movement in the former Soviet Union, or even of sympathy to feminist ideas among many women in that area, has struck many observers as odd or at least in need of explanation," say Ellen Carnaghan and Donna Bahry, two American scholars who have been studying the status of women in the post-Soviet transition. Citing the views of Russian sociologists, Carnaghan and Bahry explain,

> Where Western women want equal social treatment, Russian women reject "unfeminine" behavior and long for chivalrous males and abundant consumer goods. Where Americans debate the rights of unborn children, Russian women are more concerned with preserving their own dignity in a health care system that seems dedicated to brutalizing them. Western feminism is dismissed as a luxury only women in countries which have solved all their more pressing problems can afford.... (1994)

A similar view is expressed by Amy Tatko, who studied in Irkutsk, Siberia. The furthest thought from the minds of Russian women, says Tatko, is the concept of emancipation and feminism.

> Rather, so many of them want merely a few moments' peace and rest. They dream of sharing more time with their children and finding a few hours' personal time for themselves.... This maternal and human bond is women's savior. Amidst the hardship of work and domestic obligations and the troubles that plague so many marriages, Russian women devote themselves completely to their own children, and thus escape the need to look for alternatives and possibilities for emancipation from the underlying problems. (1993)

To cope with such hardships, women depend on and support each other to a remarkable degree. Through networks of trusted and lifelong friends, they help one another with the daily hassles of life and provide moral support in times of crisis.

Russian women are duly recognized, for whatever it's worth, on one day of the year, International Women's Day. In communist years the festival was used to emphasize the equality of sexes lacking in the capitalist West, but it remains popular today. On March 8, women are showered with gifts from their loved ones. Food stores are jammed with shoppers seeking delicacies for the traditional meal. Jewelry and gift shops stay open late, and red roses and chocolates are in high demand as Russian men make amends for how they treat their women during the rest of the year.

How does all this affect Western women traveling to Russia on business? One veteran of many visits there warns that Russian men will turn on the charm, but their basic attitude toward a female visitor will be patronizing. Her professional qualifications will be regarded initially with some skepticism, and the Western woman will have to prove herself before she will be taken seriously. But as one Russian advised, "We judge women as we judge everyone else, according to their poise, personal strength of character, and whether they demonstrate an air of authority." Indeed, Western women as well as men will be judged by their professional expertise, seriousness of purpose, cultural level, and knowledge of Russia and its history.

Another Western woman scholar with long experience in Russia suggests a few stratagems that may help women to gain recognition from Russian professional contacts. An expensive-looking business card (bilingual preferred) and an advanced degree or title will attract attention. Name-dropping will likewise impress, as will letters sent in advance by prominent persons vouching for the visitor.

Sex may also play a role in Russian contacts with Westerners. Foreign visitors, male as well as female, may find that they are objects of considerable interest to the opposite sex. Before becoming romantically involved, however, they should understand that it may be their passport rather than their personality that is the principal attraction. According to a Russian joke, a foreigner is not just a future spouse but also a means of transportation (from Russia).

Messianism

> The Occident disappears, everything collapses, everything tot-
> ters in a general conflagration: the Europe of Charlemagne and
> the Europe of the treaties of 1815, the papacy of Rome and all
> the kingdoms of the West, Catholicism and Protestantism, faith
> long lost and reason reduced to absurdity. Order becomes hence-
> forth impossible, freedom becomes henceforth impossible, and
> Occidental civilization commits suicide on top of all the ruins
> accumulated by it.... And when we see rise above this immense
> wreck this even more immense Eastern Empire like the Ark of
> the Covenant, who could doubt its mission....
> —Fyodor Tyutchev, *The Rock of Refuge*

Fyador Tyutchev, a Russian diplomat and poet, wrote those
words in 1848 in response to the liberal revolutions sweeping
Western Europe in that year. He saw Western civilization as
disintegrating while Russian civilization, morally and spiritually
superior, was rising.

Messianism is still alive in Russia today, particularly among
intellectuals, on the left as well as the right, who share a belief and pride in Russia as a great power with a special mission
in the world. Economist Mikhail F. Antonov, for example, in
an interview with *The New York Times Magazine*, showed that
Tyutchev's belief in Russia's messianic mission and superiority
was still very much alive in the 1990s.

"Let other countries surpass us in the technology of computer
production," said Antonov, "but only we can provide an answer
to the question: Why? For whose sake? We are the only legitimate
heirs to the great, spiritual Russian culture. The saving of the
world will come from Soviet Russia" (in Keller 1990, 19).

Tyutchev and Antonov epitomize Russian thinkers, past and
present, who seek to excuse the nation's material backwardness
by acclaiming correctness of cause, spiritual superiority, and
messianic mission.

"The notion of 'Holy Russia' runs deep," writes Serge Schmemann of *The New York Times*, "of a people lacking the German's

industriousness or the American's entrepreneurship, but endowed with unique spirituality and mission" (20 February 1994).

A similar view was espoused by a contemporary Russian philosopher when asked about Russia's role in the world. "Russia is European on the surface," he told me, "but deep inside it is Asian, and our link between Europe and Asia is the Russian soul. Russia's mission is to unite Europe and Asia."

Such messianic missions are not unknown to Americans, who at times have also believed that they have something special to bring to the less fortunate—Christianity to heathens, democracy to dictatorships, and the free market to state-run economies. In his State of the Union message of 1991, President George H. W. Bush also delivered a message of messianism:

> For two centuries, America has served the world as an inspiring example of freedom and democracy. For generations, America has led the struggle to preserve and extend the blessings of liberty. And today, in a rapidly changing world, American leadership is indispensable.... But we also know why the hopes of humanity turn to us. We are Americans: we have a unique responsibility to do the hard work of freedom. (*The New York Times*, 30 January 1991)

A similar note was struck ten years later by his son, President George W. Bush. In an address to the CIA on September 26, 2001, fifteen days after the terrorist attacks on the World Trade Center, the Pentagon, and the failed attempt on the Capitol, Bush said: "We're on a mission to say to the rest of the world, come with us—come with us, stand by our side to defeat the evil doers who would like to rid the world of freedom as we know it."

Americans who believe in their own mission should be sensitive to Russian messianism and fears for the future. Without great-power status, Russians fear that other countries will no longer give them the respect they are due and that Russia will lose its influence in the world. Russia's material needs, moreover, are a cause of embarrassment and a public humiliation. Russians may need aid from abroad, but they do not wish to appear as beggars seeking charity. Those who are able to provide such assistance should respect Russian sensitivities and avoid appearing as condescending.

Along with messianism, there is also a Russian tendency to blame others for their misfortunes, which has a certain logic. If Russians are indeed the chosen people and have a monopoly on truth, then others must be the cause of their misfortunes.

Freemasons and Jews, among others, have often been blamed in the past for Russia's troubles. And with nationalism resurgent, Jews are again being blamed, this time for Russia's economic ills. Indeed, as Russia goes through wrenching economic and social changes, antisemitic incidents have become more frequent among elected political leaders as well as the public at large. However, there is no official discrimination against Jews, and a poll in November 2000 by Yuri Levada, a respected Russian pollster, suggested that only 12 percent of the population had expressed openly antisemitic attitudes, which he said was about the same amount as in Europe (*Boston Globe*, 26 January 2001). Levada also believes that rabid antisemites constitute only about 3 to 4 percent of Russia's population (*San Francisco Chronicle*, 14 February 2001). When a Moscow synagogue was bombed, President Putin, in a gesture of support for Russia's Jews, visited the site and dedicated a new $22 million Jewish community center (*The New York Times*, 20 September 2000). In another symbolic gesture, Putin lit a national menorah, the traditional Jewish candelabra, to open the festival of Hanukkah 2000.

Rebellion and Revolt

> God defend you from the sight of a Russian rebellion in all its ruthless stupidity.
> —Aleksandr Pushkin, *The Captain's Daughter*

The Russians' patience sometimes wears thin and they rebel. History is replete with rebellions of serfs against masters, peasants against gentry, cossacks against lords, nobles against princes, and communists against commissars—usually with mindless destruction and wanton cruelty. There is also a record of revolt from within—palace revolutions—in the time of general secretaries and presidents as well as tsars, as Gorbachev learned in August 1991 when a junta attempted to seize power in Moscow, and as Yeltsin learned in 1993 when a similar attempt was made by hard-liners in the Russian Parliament.

Conspiracies, coups, insurrections, ethnic warfare, and national independence movements all reflect the instabilities and inequities of Russian society and its resistance to change. When peaceful evolution is not viable, revolution becomes inevitable.

Russians have long been seen as submissive to authority, politically passive, and unswerving in policy. But when the breaking point is reached, the submissive citizen spurns authority, the docile worker strikes, the passive person becomes politically active, and rigid policies are reversed almost overnight.

Such a point was reached in the late 1980s when the Soviet Union experienced food shortages, crippling strikes, a deteriorating economy, nationality unrest, ethnic warfare, movements for sovereignty or independence by the republics, inept government responses to the Chernobyl nuclear disaster and Armenian earthquake, and revelations of widespread environmental devastation.

In reaction to these events, voters of the Russian Federation rebelled in June 1991. Given a choice, they rejected the candidates of communism and chose as their president Yeltsin and his program of decentralization, democracy, and economic reform. Yeltsin thus became the first freely elected leader in Russian history. In August 1991, Russians rebelled again, taking to the streets of Moscow in a massive protest that helped bring down the old guard junta that had attempted to seize power. And in December 1995, disillusioned with reform, corruption, and a steep decline in their standard of living, Russians repudiated the Yeltsin administration by electing a parliament that was deeply divided between opponents and supporters of democratic and economic reforms, and between Westernizers and Slavophiles.

Westernizers and Slavophiles

> To Russia, in its hunger for civilization, the West seemed "the land of miracles...."
> —Thomas Masaryk, *The Spirit of Russia*

Russia's love-hate relationship with the West has given rise to proponents of two schools of thought—Westernizers and Slavophiles. Both can be regarded as Russian patriots, although they have held opposing views on Russia's position in the world.

Westernizers, recognizing Russia's backwardness, sought to borrow from the West in order to modernize. They saw Russia as a political entity that would benefit from Western enlightenment, rationalism, rule of law, technology, manufacturing, and the growth of a middle class. Among the Westernizers were political reformers, liberals, and socialists.

Slavophiles also sought to borrow from the West but were determined to protect and preserve Russia's unique cultural values and traditions. They rejected individualism and regarded the Church, rather than the state, as Russia's leading historical and moral force. As admirers of agricultural life, they were critical of urban development and industrialization. Slavophiles, moreover, sought to preserve the mir in order to prevent the growth of a Russian proletariat. They opposed socialism as alien to Russia and preferred Russian mysticism to Western rationalism. Among the Slavophiles were philosophical conservatives, nationalists, and church leaders.

The controversy between Westernizers and Slavophiles has appeared in many forms in Russian history. As Hugh Seton-Watson has pointed out, it divided Russian socialism between Marxists and Populists, Russian Marxism between Mensheviks and Bolsheviks, and Bolshevism between opponents and followers of Stalin (1952, 24). The controversy has been between those who believed in Europe and those who believed in Russia.

In our time, the conflict continues, between supporters and opponents of reform, modernizers and traditionalists, internationalists and nationalists. Today's most conservative Russians, who seek to preserve Russia's faith and harmony, are ideological descendants of the Slavophiles.

For them, the moral basis of society takes priority over individual rights and material progress, a view held today by many Russians, noncommunist as well as communist. As Solzhenitsyn said from his self-imposed seclusion in Vermont, fifteen years after his forced exile from the Soviet Union,

> There is technical progress [in the West], but this is not the same thing as the progress of humanity as such.... In Western civilization—which used to be called Western-Christian, but now might better be called Western-Pagan—along with the development of intellectual life and science there has been a loss of the serious moral basis of society. During these 300 years of Western civilization, there has been a sweeping away of duties and an expansion of rights...the only thing we have been developing is rights, rights, rights, at the expense of duty. (*Time*, 24 July 1989, 61)

That school of thought, epitomized by Solzhenitsyn, has given Russia a superiority complex toward the West in things ethereal and an inferiority complex in material matters. The West is seen as spiritually impoverished and decadent, Russia as morally rich and virtuous.

In the current environment of rapid change, Russian governments have made numerous appeals for a renewal of moral values and a search for a new "Russian idea" to embody them. President Putin has repeatedly stated that Russia's renewal depends not only on economic success or correct state policies but on a revival of moral values and national spirit, and he has called for a new "Russian idea" that emphasizes patriotism, social protections, a strong state, and great-power status. As described by Georgi Poltavchenko, one of Putin's KGB lieutenants from St. Petersburg,

> The country must have a Russian ideology! Since the Lord ordained our special path, we must also have our own ideology. The most important thing is to primarily instill patriotism and love for the motherland. Then it is the business and right of each person to have their own political views, but you must be a patriot of your own state. (2000)

That idea presumes a unique Russian way, with values superior to those of the materialistic, individualistic, and decadent West, an idea that has also been taken up by various nationalist and communist political parties.

Among those taking up the "Russian idea" are the neo-Eurasianists, who trace their roots to a movement that originated among Russian exiles in Western Europe in the early 1920s. One of the early Eurasian spokesmen, economic geographer Pyotr Savitsky, wrote in 1925:

> The idea of a Europe that combines Western and Eastern Europe is absurd.... [Eurasia] is a world apart, distinct from the countries situated on the West and [from] those situated on the South and the South-East. Russia occupies the greatest part of the Eurasian landmass; it is not divided between two continents but forms a third, independent geographic entity. (in Thom 1994, 66)

Today's Eurasianists, who have a home in Russia's Eurasian Party, also reject the West and see Russia's future in the East. They advocate a union of the three Slavic peoples—Russians, Belarusians, and Ukrainians—and a federation of the Slavic peoples with their Turkic neighbors to the south and east in a political union that looks strikingly similar to the former Soviet Union, and with the Russians in charge. But there are also politicians with Eurasianist views in other political parties, among the more prominent of whom are Gennadi Zyuganov, leader of the Russian Communist Party, and Vladimir Zhirinovsky, the ultranationalist leader of the so-called Liberal Democratic Party. In the March 2000 presidential election, Zyuganov received 29.2 percent of the vote and Zhirinosvky, 2.7 percent, a far cry from the 1993 parliamentary elections when his party surprisingly won almost one-fourth of the vote.

4

State and Society

With the mind alone Russia cannot be understood,
No ordinary yardstick spans her greatness;
She stands alone, unique-
In Russia one can only believe.

—Fyodor Tyutchev

The Russian Heritage

If men could foresee the future, they would still behave as they
do now.

—Russian proverb

"I have seen the future and it works," wrote an American writer
after visiting Russia in 1919. This euphoric vision, attributed to
journalist and author Lincoln Steffens, we now know was twice
mistaken. The Soviet state did not portend the future, and Soviet
society did not work.

To be sure, state and society were turned upside down by the
Great October Revolution—as communists call the Bolshevik
seizure of power in 1917. The small, French-speaking elite that
had ruled Russia was removed from power by confiscation of
land and property, exile, or outright murder. In theory, the new
ruling class was to be workers and peasants, represented by lo-

cal Soviets (councils) and guided by the Communist Party. In practice, however, after Joseph Stalin had eliminated his rivals, one autocracy was replaced by another.

Building on the utopian dreams of generations of Russian thinkers, the Bolsheviks planned to create a new state—and a new "Soviet person"—that would correct all of old Russia's inequities. By applying the principles of what they called "scientific socialism"—a Western import—they would establish the new order by nationalizing production, instituting central planning, abolishing private property, and redistributing wealth according to the Marxist maxim as modified by the Soviets, "From each according to his capacities, to each according to his work." And all this was to be accomplished under the direction of the Communist Party which, as the Soviet Constitution put it, would be "the leading and guiding force of Soviet society and the nucleus of its political system."

The Bolsheviks, however, found themselves heirs to many relics of old Russia—a vast multinational empire dominated by Russians, governed from its center, and ruled by coercion rather than law; a state-imposed ideology that set standards for citizen behavior; a bureaucracy that was arrogant, corrupt, and incompetent; the priority of the community over the individual; a pervasive censorship; suspicion of dissidents and others who thought differently from the state; and a ubiquitous secret police to enforce the state's will.

Americans who rail against the intrusions of government in their lives should try to imagine a state and society that is run like a huge corporation without competitors, a monopoly controlled and managed by insiders. In this corporation, individual rights were subordinated to the greater communal good, as seen by the board of directors, whose decisions were final.

The United States also had a revolution, but it did not turn the social structure upside down. Its population was homogeneous, mostly of English origin at the time of the revolution, numbering only two million and living in relative proximity along the Atlantic coast. The system of governance, based on

English common law, economic liberalism, and individual rights, did portend the future, and it worked. America's models were England and Western enlightenment. The models for Russia were Byzantium and Mongol rule.

Today's Russia, neither European nor Asian, has also inherited the problems of the past. In many ways it is a developed country, with heavy industry, high technology, world-class science, an educated populace, formidable military strength, and nuclear power. In other ways it is a developing country, with poverty, inefficiency, low productivity, poor public health, a primitive infrastructure, and a disregard for the rule of law. It is that Third-World Russia that reformers are attempting to coax into the modern world.

Experts, both Russian and Western, are divided on Russia's prospects for reform. But whatever the results, they can be expected to reflect the values and views that are deeply rooted in the Russian past. Much as the Soviet Union retained many key elements of the Russian past, so too will the new Russia, in many ways, resemble the old. As an economist in Prague has written, "Top-down imposition of socialism ended in failure. Let's wait and see how top-down imposition of capitalism will end" (Vasko 1977, 105).

Statism

> Who serves the Tsar cannot serve the people.
>
> —Russian proverb

Russians have a strong and abiding suspicion of government. Recent public opinion polls show that the vast majority of Russians are convinced that most of their leaders hold public office only for personal gain and do not care about the concerns of the common man. This estrangement from government runs very deep and is based, in part, on past experience.

In the past, Russian governments have served rulers rather than the ruled. Until Russia's free elections of 1991, democratic governance was experienced only once, in 1917, during the brief period between the democratic February revolution and the Bolshevik October Revolution. With those exceptions, authoritarianism has been the rule in Russian governance.

"There is little in the country's past," writes Robert G. Kaiser,

> that has prepared it to become a modern, tolerant, and efficient democracy. Russians have no real experience with independent civic institutions, checks and balances, or even the restrained use of power. Russian citizens have been estranged from the state for many centuries.... (2001)

For centuries, Russia was an absolute monarchy, ruled as a paramilitary garrison state to guard against threats both internal and external. As George Vernadsky, Yale University's distinguished professor of Russian history, described it, "In the Tsardom of Moscow of the sixteenth and seventeenth centuries we find an entirely new concept of society and its relation to the state. All the classes of the nation, from top to bottom, except the slaves, were bound to the service of the state..." (1953, 337). That state, moreover, was ruled by hereditary tsars who held absolute power, issuing decrees which had the force of law. The Russian *ukaz* (decree) has come into English as *ukase*, a decree having force of law. In the 1990s, Boris Yeltsin also ruled by decree, as tsars and commissars had done before him; and Vladimir Putin, Russia's new president, also has extraordinary powers under the Constitution of 1993. As Yuri Afanasyev, a leading reformer in the 1980s, put it,

> It was and is characteristic of Russia to have the people at the "bottom" harshly subordinated to the people at the "top," and for people generally to be subordinated to the state; such relations were formed back in the twelfth century. The eternal oppression in Russia created a reaction against it of intolerance, aggression, and hostility; and it is this oppression and the reaction to it that create cruelty and mass violence. (1991, 38)

Russia's rulers, perceiving domestic unrest and political dissent as threats to their ability to govern a vast empire, have not hesitated to use force to maintain their authority. They saw Russia surrounded by hostile or unstable powers, and they took advantage of any weakness or instability along their state's periphery to secure its borders and extend its territorial reach.

With power concentrated at the center, the influence of the state on Russian society has been pervasive. In old Russia, the largest landholders were the crown, church, and aristocracy. Many sectors of the economy were controlled or subsidized by the state. For both rulers and the ruled, service to the state was the primary duty.

In the Soviet era, the state played an even larger role. Moscow's heavy hand was found in the economy, culture, education, the media, religion, and citizens' private lives—planning, directing, instructing, and stifling initiative in the process. Big Brother—or rather Big Daddy, in a paternalistic society—was everywhere. Russians, moreover, have often idolized their leaders. The tsar was seen as the *tsar-batyushka* (tsar-father). Stalin was similarly adored as a father figure. And President Putin, unknown prior to being named by Yeltsin as his successor, regularly receives approval ratings of more than 70 percent.

Commenting on Russian governance, George F. Kennan has written,

> Forms of government and the habits of governments tend over the long run to reflect the understandings and expectations of their peoples. The Russian people...have never known democracy as we understand it. They have experienced next to nothing of the centuries-long development of the discipline of self-government out of which our own political culture has evolved. (1989, 38)

The result has been a submissive citizenry, accustomed to—indeed expecting—direction from above, being told what to do and what to think. "It is difficult for us to make decisions," a Russian psychologist told me. "We are so used to being told what to do that we cannot take the initiative and decide for ourselves." Such an attitude helps to explain the reluctance of individual Russians to become involved in issues which they believe are the responsibility of government and where the role of the individual citizen seems insignificant.

Another centuries-old tradition is a state-sanctioned ideology that serves as a moral guide, determining what is right and wrong. In the tsarist era, the ideology was Russian Orthodoxy, the state religion. In the Soviet period, the Communist Party imposed its own standards of cultural, moral, and political behavior. Today, Russia is searching for a new ideology, a "Russian idea" to provide moral guidance.

The contrasts between Russia and the United States are again apparent. In the latter, state power has been limited and diffused, both within the federal government and between federal and state authorities. Free elections and a multiparty system have ensured representation of the popular will. A government role in culture and the media has been eschewed. Church and state have been separate and the rights of religious minorities protected. The development of moral and cultural values has been left to private institutions independent of government—the churches, the media, universities, and that typically American institution, the private voluntary organization. An economy based on private property and the free market, although at times assisted and regulated by government, has remained free from state control.

The Bureaucracy

> More than in any other country, officials in Russia considered themselves a superior species, appointed to drive the herds of human cattle. Obedience and patience were required of the cattle, willingness to wait for hours and days for a decision, and acceptance of the decision when given.
> —Hugh Seton-Watson, *The Decline of Imperial Russia*

In his description of Russian officials, the British historian Hugh Seton-Watson was writing about nineteenth-century Russia. His words, however, would be equally valid for the Russia of our time, when the tradition of an omnipotent, obstinate, and obstruction-ist bureaucracy still obtains. Foreign visitors who interact with Russians will need to understand this bureaucracy and learn how to deal with it.

A diplomatic colleague of mine who had previously served in Iran and Syria told me that after his posting to Moscow he felt very much at home. As in the Middle East, he explained, papers went from desk to desk in the bureaucracy, responsibility was diluted, and decisions were referred to higher-ups. (He might have added that such behavior is not limited to Russia and the Middle East but is also found in most developing countries.)

Before proceeding with joint endeavors, visitors will need the approval of all the government agencies involved, which is easier said than done. Doing business in Russia, explained John Blaney, a former economics counselor at the American Embassy in Moscow, is "almost like a three-dimensional chess game, where each level has different rules and different pieces, and every once in a while, on any level, all the rules change" (*The New York Times*, 23 March 1991).

Some Russian officials, to be sure, are creative, decisive, and motivated and could easily hold their own in London's "City" or on New York City's Wall Street. They are exceptions, however, and stand out among the others. Many of today's officials whom foreigners will meet—"dead souls," they are called in Russian—prefer to follow established practice rather than show initiative and risk making errors that might put their careers as risk. Under the communists, initiative was not rewarded, and most of today's officials are holdovers from the communist past.

The result is rigidity, incompetence, sloth, conservatism, and a tendency to avoid responsibility by passing the buck to higher-ups. Supervisory officials, moreover, are responsible for the errors of their underlings and can be severely disciplined when mistakes are made. What to do?

As one veteran Russian interpreter advised me, "Foreign-ers should understand that many Russian officials they will do business with are incompetent and hold their jobs only because of nepotism, friendships, or former Party membership. Visitors should try in advance to get the names of competent officials and seek them out." That can be done with a little home-work—contacting colleagues who have previously negotiated with the officialdom and learned which officials to seek out and which to avoid.

At the higher levels of the bureaucracy during the communist era there were the *nomenklatura*, the lifelong, tenured positions filled by Communist Party appointees on the basis of political reliability. Wielding unchallenged power, the nomenklatura had a vested interest in maintaining the status quo and was positioned to block or slow change. That elite had its own lifestyle—better housing, access to special "closed stores" and upscale vacation resorts, superior medical care, and the highest award for loyalty, foreign travel. With the collapse of communism, the nomenklatura was expected to disappear, but like many other elements of Russian society it has reappeared with many of the same perks.

Today's nomenklatura, many of them holdovers from the Soviet era, also has free housing, free medical care in the best clinics and hospitals, vacations at resorts formerly reserved for the Soviet elite, cars, weekend dachas, and many other privileges (*The New York Times*, 23 May 1995). But instead of stealing from the state under cover, they now do it openly.

Among today's privileged are also the privatizers, the "new rich," as well as the government officials whose cooperation they buy with bribes. The perks of this moneyed class are also little different from those of the old nomenklatura—luxury goods, quality housing and medical care, superior schooling for their children, foreign travel and possession of wealth outside Russia, and freedom from constraints of the law. The only forces influencing the behavior of this new class, says Russian law professor Sergei Shishkin, are ties of loyalty, friendship, and trust among its members (1994).

Bureaucrats today still issue licenses and permits, control municipal housing and land transfers for commercial and other uses, set export quotas for various commodities, and give approvals for new businesses. They are poorly paid, their morale is low, opportunities for corruption are everywhere, and the old Russian tradition of stealing from the state continues. Some refer to the new Russia today as a "kleptocracy."

How should visitors deal with these officials whose approval will be needed for joint endeavors? First, open discussions as high in the chain of command as possible. Decisions on foreign proposals are rarely made at the working level but are usually referred to more senior officials. The higher one starts, the closer one will be to the person who can make decisions. Indeed, when petitioners are able to state their case directly to an official with authority, decisions are made more promptly, if not immediately. But that presents another challenge—to determine who has the authority and who decides.

Prepare the groundwork by presenting in advance a paper outlining your proposal. That will give the bureaucracy time to study the offer, check it out with higher officials, and give you a more authoritative response. Such a paper will also help to ensure that the proposal is accurately presented as it works its way up through the bureaucracy. To conform with the Russian approach (the concept first and then the details), begin the paper with a general introduction—the background, history, and even philosophy behind the proposal—before proceeding to the particulars.

An initial *nyet* should not be accepted as a definitive response. Russians can change positions when they know more about a proposal and are persuaded that it is in their interest. Keep talking. Negotiations may be lengthy and decisions slow in coming (see chapter 6, "Negotiating with Russians"). Everything takes longer in Russia and requires patience and perseverance.

Germans, who have been doing business with Russia for centuries, have learned from experience. "Many American businessmen," says one German banker, "come to Moscow and leave three weeks later completely frustrated. German businessmen are willing to stay six months to make a deal" (Protzman 1989).

One reason why things take longer is that Russians feel more comfortable with persons they have known for some time. The familiar face is welcome, and repeated visits to Russia may be necessary before confidence and trust are built.

Gift giving is an old Eastern custom. In Slavic lands visitors have been traditionally welcomed with gifts of bread and salt, the staples of life, as the U.S. astronauts were when they docked with the Russian space station *Mir* in June 1995. (The Americans brought flowers and chocolates.)

The tradition of exchanging gifts continues, but the staples of life have changed. Bribes are illegal, of course, but between a gift and a bribe there is a narrow line that may be difficult to discern. In any event, the gift of a VCR, computer, or stereo system will grease the wheels—as well as the palms—of the bureaucracy. Less costly items will also be appreciated—new video films, popular music cassettes, electronic gadgets, Scotch whiskey, and almost anything Western. Women will be grateful for perfume, cosmetics, costume jewelry, chocolates, and fancy soaps. Good tea is always appreciated but in bulk rather than tea bags.

Bring a bag of souvenirs, especially those with a university, company, or city logo. Russians are avid collectors of souvenir pins. And in a nation of bibliophiles, books are treasured. Particularly welcome are recent publications by well-known authors, but almost anything new in English will do.

Breaking bread breaks barriers. Russians welcome invitations to lunch or dinner where business can be conducted informally and where they will not be speaking "on the record." The working breakfast, however, is alien to Russian culture and is not yet in vogue. Visitors from abroad may be invited to Russian homes now that the risk of association with foreigners is gone. Favors are appreciated and will be reciprocated.

The greatest favor would be a much-prized invitation to visit a foreign country, with costs covered by the host. Russians have an enormous interest in foreign travel, but in the Soviet period travel was limited to a favored few. Now it is much easier to obtain a Russian passport and exit visa, although getting a foreign visa may be more difficult, because screening procedures have been tightened by some countries.

Contacts with the bureaucracy have increased, but many visitors wonder why they seldom see papers on desks in the offices where they are received. This is because many of the higher officials have two offices—one for work and another for receiving visitors.

Crime and Corruption

It's easy to steal when seven others are stealing.
                                        —Russian proverb

As in many Eastern societies, what counts is not what you know but *whom* you know, and often whom you pay off. *Blat* (influence or pull) is a way of life in Russia, along with its first cousin, nepotism. Officials have long been accustomed to using their positions to help themselves, their families, and friends. But today, for most citizens, corruption is a way of life. A discreet gift will bring favorable treatment in government offices. Knowing the right person can mean getting an apartment or gaining admission to a preferred school or university. Bribery can get a young man an exemption from military service.

Everything is for sale for the right price. Tax breaks are sold for dollars; timber rights are given in exchange for Western cars; criminal investigations are halted for payoffs; federal funds are deposited in certain banks in exchange for bribes; property leases are extended for cash; police protection is sold for bribes. Managers loot their firms by not paying bills and sending their capital abroad. The list goes on and on.

"Bribes used to be given in envelopes," said one Russian. "Now they are given in cartons," a reference not only to inflation but to the increase in the amount of the bribes. One American contractor who works in Russia describes the bribes

80

he must pay there as "solicited gratuities, an accepted cost of doing business."

Bribery and embezzlement were common in old Russia, as Nikolai Gogol told us in his comic classic, *The Inspector General*. They were also common in the Soviet era, although seldom brought to light, and definitely not the subject of literature. Under glasnost, however, after former President Mikhail Gorbachev assumed power in 1985, an epidemic of corruption in high places was exposed and offenders were brought to trial. In one of those trials, Leonid Brezhnev's son-in-law, Yuri Churbanov, received a twelve-year sentence for bribery in the cover-up of widespread corruption by the highest communist officials in Uzbekistan. And in 1990, the regional Party chief of Volgograd and fourteen other local Party leaders there resigned as a result of public outrage over charges that they had helped friends and relatives to get apartments. Volgograd citizens without connections had to wait up to fifteen years for scarce apartments (*Washington Post*, 6 March 1990).

Among the more recent cases that have been publicized in the world press are charges of money laundering by Russians through foreign banks, allegations that President Yeltsin and his family received bribes from a Swiss company for lucrative Kremlin construction contracts, and reports that thousands of well-connected Russian officials reaped huge profits from the sale of government bonds a few days before Russia's financial collapse in 1998.

Most disconcerting to Russians is that this type of illicit behavior, long practiced by officials, has now spread throughout the population and become a way of life. Traffic police take bribes from motorists; teachers are paid to give students good grades; professors sell admission to top universities; and doctors in state-run hospitals demand payment for supposedly free care before treating patients. Almost anything can be "bought" with a payoff—to low officials as well as high.

Paying taxes is a new civic responsibility for Russians, and it is a responsibility for which the past years of a centrally planned economy has not prepared them. Consequently, tax collection has been a problem for every Russian government since 1991, although President Putin on January 1, 2001, made it easier by introducing a flat tax of 13 percent on income. As French economist Yves Gisse explains,

> A population that has been accustomed to receive free public services and other state support and not to pay new income taxes nor indirect taxes will have difficulties to establish a strong tax administration system responsible for collecting personal and corporate taxes at the country level. There again, it is a matter of a new cultural adaptation to economic change. (1997, 307)

Corruption has also become a way of doing business in the private sector. The key players are government officials who issue licenses for new businesses and control natural resources, traders and financiers who can move money and goods around, and protection racketeers who are hired to ensure that business deals are honored. Unfortunately, corruption is a means of survival for underpaid officials seeking to support their families on meager salaries.

Crime has also risen sharply in Russia, with major increases reported for consumer cheating, evasion of customs duties, drug trafficking, theft of arms and munitions, and apartment robberies. The increased crime is very troubling to Russians, and public opinion polls show that they place it high on their list of greatest grievances. Russians assume that everything and everyone have been bought, and as a consequence, they do not trust anyone outside their immediate circle of family and friends. Their prime motivation appears to be how to protect and benefit their own family in these trying times. "Most Russians," says the *Economist*, "would still rather pay up or shut up than kick up a fuss" (*Economist* [UK] 1–7 December 2001).

Also troubling are the machinations of the mafia.

The Mafia

> Organized crime has supplanted many of the functions of the
> state. A coalition of organized crime and former Party elites
> provides the ruling elites of many regions of Russia and many
> other CIS states. Organized crime provides many of the services
> that citizens expect from their state—protection of commercial
> businesses, employment for citizens, mediation in disputes. Pri-
> vate security, often run by organized crime, is replacing state
> law enforcement.
>
> —Louise I. Shelley, *Demokratizatsiya*

Mafia is the term used by Russians to describe the vast network
of gangsters and racketeers who are said to control much of
the Russian economy, including private businesses, banks, and
markets, and who are responsible for much of the violence that
permeates society. According to official Russian sources, more
than nine thousand criminal organizations are believed to be
operating inside the country, employing nearly one hundred thousand people. Newcomers to Russia should be aware, though, that
Russians apply the term *mafia* indiscriminately, using it also to
describe legitimate entrepreneurs and others who have achieved
financial success in the new Russia.

Russia is difficult to imagine. In 2001, more than 34,000
murders were recorded, and an additional 30,000 people were
reported missing (*Asia Times*, 21 May 2002). Most murders are
the result of domestic violence, but contract killings are also a
major problem, and victims are mostly businesspeople. "Murders,
kidnappings, assaults and robberies are becoming virtually everyday occurrences," said President Putin at a meeting on crime
in May 2002 (*Asia Times*). Russia and the world were shocked
when Duma Deputy Galina Starovoitova was gunned down in
St. Petersburg in 1998, a killing that, three years later, still had
not been solved (*St. Petersburg Times*, 25 June 1999).

Russian victims are usually businessmen or higher income
people. According to the Russian Ministry of Interior, contract
killings have been increasing; 599 businessmen were slain in

1998 on orders of their competitors. Contract killings mostly "hit" midlevel officials in the oil and gas, metals, and banking sectors. Foreign businessmen and Russian highflyers have rarely been targeted, but judges are intimidated, and prosecutors and investigative journalists have been assassinated.

The mafia consists of regionally or market-based criminal groups, distinct from each other but linked by cooperative arrangements. They began by controlling illegal activities—gambling, prostitution, stolen cars, and narcotics—before branching out and spreading their influence over virtually all aspects of Russian private life and reaching abroad to Western Europe, the United States, and Israel. The Russian mafia extorts money—and in some cases demands a share in ownership—from small privately owned businesses as well as banks, large businesses, and even some of the new Western-built hotels frequented by foreign visitors. One of the mafia's main activities is to provide the protection that private property owners require but are unable to obtain from the legitimate authorities.* Through its international contacts, the mafia is also engaged in the illegal export of oil and other commodities, the smuggling of weapons and nuclear materials, the laundering of money, and the flight of much-needed capital abroad.

The Russian mafia's roots are not in Italy (whence comes the word *mafia*) but rather in the Soviet political system, which exercised power through criminality and violence. In this sense, the mafia has replaced the Communist Party by providing "order" in Russia. Indeed, the mafia is believed to be an alliance between criminals and former communists in the state bureaucracy, including the KGB, which has supplied many of the mafia's strong-arm henchmen.

Organized crime in Russia and the other states of the former Soviet Union inhibits the growth of democracy, corrupts do-

---

* Much of the material here on the mafia is derived from *Democratizatsiya, The Journal of Post-Soviet Democratization* 2, no. 3 (Summer 1994).

mestic politics, discourages foreign investment and economic assistance, depletes natural resources, and deprives domestic economies of capital. Unless curbed, it will be a festering threat to Russia's future.

The most disturbing aspect of mafia activity in Russia, says Marshall Goldman, "is that a growing number of Russians have come to believe that this distorted form of mafia control is what a free market system means" (1995).

The KGB

> I am giving away no secrets when I reveal that the new Russian intelligence service is pretty much the old KGB in drag.
> —John le Carré, "My New Friends in Russia"

One part of the Russian bureaucracy that works well is the successor organizations to the KGB of the Soviet era. The new Foreign Intelligence Service (SVR) has inherited the foreign intelligence components of the KGB, while the Federal Security Service (FSB), formerly the Federal Counterintelligence Service (FSK), is responsible for internal security. A third successor, the Main Guard Administration (GUO), has responsibility for the president's personal security and the security of the Kremlin. The acronyms have changed, but these agencies are all commonly known to Russians as the KGB, and they do much of the same work. Indeed, their officers today still refer to themselves as *Chekists*, after *Cheka* (the Extraordinary Committee against Sabotage and Counter-Revolution), the name of the secret police organization founded in 1917 by Felix Dzerzhinsky, one of the original Bolsheviks.

KGB activities abroad are well known to Westerners through films and novels as well as news reports. Less known abroad are its domestic responsibilities, which are embodied in legislation confirmed by President Yeltsin in April 1995. These include combating organized crime, creating enterprises as fronts for investigative work, controlling state secrets, operating its own prison system, and providing security for the armed forces and the federal government (*The New York Times*, 7 April 1995).

The KGB's mandate is broad, and so are its activities. Indeed, it is said that in Russia today it is difficult to do anything in business without some arrangement with the KGB, especially since many of President Putin's senior appointees are former KGB officers. As a Russian journalist describes it,

> The KGB was not just the Soviet Union's most powerful institution, but also was *and is* [emphasis added] a corporation with its own, quite specific organizational culture that is driven by notions of the imperial state and disrespect for individual lives, freedoms and liberties. (Albats 2001)

Russia has had a secret police since the sixteenth century, when Tsar Ivan the Terrible established his *Oprichnina* to root out political opposition. The name has changed over the centuries, and the scope of its activities has expanded considerably, but its essential purpose has not changed. Russian rulers have continued to maintain a secret police to counter domestic opposition and to enforce their will. As the twenty-first century opens, Russia's democratically elected leaders recognize that they too need a security agency.

The KGB was Stalin's personal instrument for carrying out his reign of terror. According to a former KGB officer, material in KGB archives has disclosed that eighteen million people were "repressed" from 1935 to 1945—about seven million of whom were shot. These figures, however, do not include deaths in prison and labor camps or by means of execution other than shooting. Many historians, Russian as well as Western, believe that deaths due to the reign of terror were far greater, approaching even more than the twenty million Soviets citizens who died in World War II (*The New York Times*, 14 February 1990).

Whatever the number, Stalin's abuses were extensive, and there is hardly a family, especially among the more educated, that was not in some way a victim. Today, with the KGB no longer the feared instrument of the past, Russians will not hesitate to tell visitors what their family members experienced during the terror.

Many of the Russian officials serving abroad or at home in state agencies having contact with foreigners are KGB officers, or they have been co-opted by the KGB to report on their foreign contacts. Foreigners working with Russians will likely encounter such personnel at some point, although they may not be aware of it.

Encounters with KGB officers of Russia need not be a cause of concern. KGB personnel who serve abroad are among the best and brightest. Intelligence, like science, draws talent. Members of the KGB's First Directorate (foreign intelligence) are often the sons of privileged members of the nomenklatura. They are also likely to be intelligent—as well as intelligence—officers who demonstrate flexibility, initiative, and confidence in dealing with foreigners. Moreover, those who have served abroad have the knowledge and experience of the West that most Russians lack. Today, in addition to military and political intelligence, their priorities may also include gathering economic and technological data, but they will also be collecting and reporting information on people they meet.

What is the KGB looking for? Of interest are personal foibles and weaknesses that might be used for blackmail at some future time—unusual lifestyles, addictions, sexual preferences, and financial difficulties. Foreign visitors to Russia are no longer routinely followed, but hotel rooms and telephones may still be bugged and mail monitored. Any suspicious activity can be expected to attract KGB interest. And the KGB has a long memory. Once an item goes into a person's dossier, it may lie dormant for many years, only to surface when an earlier indiscretion has been long forgotten and the individual in question has reached a position of importance.

A warm, personal relationship with a Russian, however, can thwart even the KGB. A former American exchange student in Russia relates how he was assigned to share a dormitory room with a Russian student. Entering his room one day, the

American found his roommate amorously involved with a female visitor. "Disappear," growled the Russian. The American quickly retreated but stationed himself outside the door and prevented others from entering the room until the liaison had been concluded. In appreciation, the Russian confessed that he had been assigned by the KGB to report on his roommate. "But since you are such a fine fellow," he added, "just stay in your room and study for a few nights, and I'll say in my report that you are a serious scholar and not a CIA spy."

One final word of caution. Visitors to Russia should not say anything in public—or in a place where it might be overheard—that could get a citizen in trouble with the authorities. Never mention to others the names of friends whose actions or views might make difficulties for them. When Russians trust someone, they will open up and tell everything, but they will also expect that person to respect the confidence.

The Law

If all laws perished, the people would live in truth and justice.
—Russian proverb

When Richard Nixon named his cabinet after winning the presidential election of 1968, a prominent Russian law professor asked me why so many lawyers had been chosen by the new president. Lawyers in the Soviet Union did not have much prestige, and Russians were puzzled by the prominence of lawyers in U.S. public life.

Lawyers in the Soviet Union had little social status or political influence, had little importance in the legal system, and were poorly paid. More important than training in the law was a position in the Communist Party. With the exception of Gorbachev and Lenin, who both studied law, Soviet political leaders have usually been engineers by training. Yeltsin's education and work experience, for example, was in construction engineering, and President Putin, although he studied law, made his career in the

KGB. That has been changing in the new Russia as owners of private property have found that they need lawyers.

In response to the professor's question, I first cited the trite but true textbook response that the United States has a government of laws and not of men. I next discussed the significance of private property in U.S. law and the importance of the contract, both of which may require lawyers. My third explanation—more meaningful in the Russian context—concerned the concept of compromise, the foundation of democracy. I explained that in U.S. civil disputes, most lawyers settle their cases through negotiation and compromise; and in criminal law, most charges are settled through plea bargaining—a compromise between lawyers for the state and for the defense. The meaning was not lost on the professor because *kompromis*, in Russian, has a pejorative meaning and is considered a sign of weakness and a breach of faith.

More important than the law in Russian culture are truth and justice. The search for social justice is a continuing theme in Russian literature, from Tolstoy to Solzhenitsyn. Russian writers, reflecting their quest for social justice and universal harmony, have regretted their country's failure to assuage suffering and eliminate inequities.

"Bolshevism," wrote Nikolai Berdyaev, "showed itself to be much more faithful to certain primordial Russian traditions, to the Russian search for universal social justice…and to the Russian method of government and control by coercion" (1960, 113). Berdyaev, a prominent religious philosopher, had a youthful flirtation with Marxism but later became a strong critic of Bolshevism. Expelled from the Soviet Union in 1922, he settled in Paris.

For Russians, the consensus of the community has been more important than the legalisms of the law. Not surprisingly, Russians discount the ability of law to provide the truth and justice they seek.

In the mir the rule of law did not apply. Decisions were made by the village assembly and based on what made sense at the time and appeared just and useful for the common good. Crime was not considered by peasants in the abstract, as Nicholas Vakar has noted. Stealing wood from the state or a landowner, for example, was against the law but was not considered by peasants to be a crime. But stealing even the smallest object from a fellow villager or the commune would bring the culprit a severe beating, at the very least, or even mutilation or death. And the horse thief, as in the American West, was one of society's worst enemies. If caught, he was promptly tortured and lynched without trial. The same was true for arsonists in a land where thatched huts burned quickly and an entire village could be rapidly destroyed by fire (1962, 75).

In tsarist Russia, rule was by imperial decree, and the tsar's will was not subject to law. As Richard Wortman writes, "The tsarist state, ever insistent on the supremacy of the executive power, has held the judicial system in disdain, and this disdain was shared by the officialdom and the nobility" (1976, 3).

Soviet leaders continued the tradition of being above the law. In the 1960s, when they mounted a campaign against foreign-currency speculators, several suspects were arrested and, in accordance with the Soviet penal code, were sentenced to long terms of imprisonment. Public opinion, however, whipped up by press reports on the speculators' high lifestyles, demanded the death penalty.

Nikita Khrushchev, Party chief at the time, summoned the public prosecutor general and demanded the death sentence. When told that Soviet law did not permit execution for currency speculation, Khrushchev replied, "Who's the boss: we or the law? We are masters over the law; not the law over us—so we have to change the law...." A law was indeed passed, providing the death penalty for speculating in large sums of foreign currency, and the speculators were tried, some for a second time, sentenced to death, and executed (in Simis 1982, 29–31).

Russian and Western law have a common ancestry in Roman law. Indeed, in the year 1000, writes U.S. legal scholar Harold Berman, the law of Kievan Rus was similar to that of Germanic Europe and Anglo-Saxon England. But the Franks converted to Christianity in 486, Kievan Rus not until 988, and this put Russia five hundred years behind the West in the development of its legal system (1963, 191–93).

Differences between Russian and Western law derive from Byzantium and Russian Orthodoxy. In Byzantium, the emperor had absolute authority over justice, making and unmaking laws, legislating on religious as well as civil matters, and acting as supreme judge of the land. In Byzantium, moreover, church and state were one, and the emperor was presumed to have the obligation to monitor the morals of his people. Russian law, accordingly, has been more intrusive in personal lives. The Orthodox Church and Russian law have also emphasized community and a common sense of brotherhood and togetherness. This, says Berman, has given Russian law

> a strong tradition of collective social consciousness which relies for its motivation less on reason than on common faith and common worship, and which finds expression less in legal formality and "due process" than in more spontaneous and more impulsive responses. (222)

Moreover, adds Berman, there is a Russian belief that large areas of life remain outside the law,

> particularly in…politics and policymaking, where reliance is placed on the nonrational, non-legal factors of force and violence, on the one hand, and of moral unity and common faith on the other. The personality of rulers still plays a dominant role; personal influence is a crucial factor in impeding the movement for stability of laws. (270)

Western legalism and its time-consuming commitment to "due process" have been disdained by many of Russia's intelligentsia, who have looked to personal and administrative relationships rather than to the formality of the law. As Nina Khrushcheva describes it,

Such a country [Russia] established a set of values in mirror opposition to the West: Russian charity versus Western justice; order vs. law; trust vs. responsibility; nihilism and negation vs. competition; humanity vs. professionalism; truth vs. rules; faith vs. stimulus purpose; universalism vs. individualism; spirituality vs. interests, etc. (2000/2001, 48)

Attempts in the late nineteenth and early twentieth centuries to establish a *Rechtsstaat*, a law-based state—Russians still use the German term—were only partially successful, due in part to the power of the tsar and a long tradition of arbitrary rule in disregard of the law. That tradition continued during the Soviet period, when the state issued thousands of administrative regulations which were enforced by the authorities and the courts, although many of them violated the laws of the land. The Soviet judicial system, moreover, was subservient to the state, and a court's decision, particularly in the provinces, was often influenced by a telephone call to the presiding judge from a local Communist Party official, a practice known as "telephone law."

In civil law, a citizen could generally expect a fair trial, although the interests of the state were often given priority. In criminal law, however, acquittals were rare. As in Western Europe, but unlike the United States and the United Kingdom, a trial was required in Russia even if the accused pleaded guilty, as he or she did in some 90 percent of the cases. Of the remaining cases, only about one in ten resulted in acquittal. The judge, assisted by two assessors (lay judges), played a stronger role than in American or British courts, acting as an interrogator together with the prosecutor, rather than as a neutral umpire. In criminal law, until new legislation was passed in 1989, defense lawyers were often unable to obtain access to imprisoned defendants and their court records.

In Russia, endless exceptions to the law have been allowed that permit the outcome sought by the courts and the state. Many laws are poorly drafted and vague. Also less than clear are the details of their operation, which are subject to administra-

92

tive regulation. Laws are often passed but not enforced and are
frequently overtaken by new legislation.

One aspect of the law where Russian and Western differences are most striking is that of individual rights. In the West
these rights are based on constitutions and laws that spell out
the individual's rights and limit state infringement on them.
To Russians, however, rigorous application of the law to defend
individuals may appear unduly legalistic. They would rather judge
each situation in the light of circumstances, as in the mir, and
weigh the relative interests of the individual and the community,
a contest in which community interests may prevail.

Individual rights, moreover, may clash with the communal
ethic. Russians are prejudiced against those who live differently or
better than their neighbors. And in a culture that values harmony
of thought and communal good, persons who differ from the established order are suspect. *Individualysty* (individualists)—which
has a pejorative meaning in Russian—appear opposed to the
sense of community as the basis for social good.

In Russia today there is again talk of a Rechtsstaat, and progress in achieving it has been enhanced by a program of judicial
reform personally promoted by President Putin and approved
by the State Duma in November 2001 with the support of all
political parties.[†] The reforms affect all of the courts, including
the *arbitrazh* (commercial) courts that deal with disputes between
firms and between firms and the government.

The new legislation is intended to strengthen the independence and authority of judges, many of whom have been regarded
as incompetent and subject to outside pressures, while also reducing their immunity from prosecution and making them subject
to discipline. Appointments of judges will no longer be screened
by local legislatures—a procedure that made judges subject to

---

[†] In this treatment of judicial reform, the author has drawn from
Peter H. Solomon Jr., *Fixing the Courts in Russia? The Putin/Kozak
Reforms of 2001* (Cambridge, MA: Cambridge Energy Research
Associates, 2001).

influence by local politicians and their wealthy friends—but by a qualification commission of judges, lawyers, legal scholars, and Kremlin officials who will review appointments, promotions, removals from office, and punishments. Except for those of the constitutional courts, judges will be appointed not for unlimited terms, as previously, but for six-year terms, and the same person will not be allowed to be appointed as presiding or deputy presiding judge in the same court more than twice in a row.

Judges will also be forced to retire at age sixty-five for regular courts and seventy for higher courts. Furthermore, they can be disciplined and face criminal charges or administrative punishment at the request of the prosecutor general and, if so decided, by a panel of three Supreme Court judges and with the consent of the Supreme Qualification Commission. To inhibit bribery, a dramatic increase in funding will provide judges with higher salaries, additional staff, computerization of court proceedings, repair of court buildings, and interest-free and forgivable loans to enable new judges to buy homes.

The reforms also propose to establish nationwide, by the year 2003, trials by ten-member juries for major crimes while empowering judges to hear ordinary criminal cases on their own. Judges, however, will still have the power to overturn jury verdicts. The "lay assessors," who sat with judges on the bench during the Soviet era but had little influence on verdicts and sentences, will be eliminated.

The new legislation also introduces other reforms intended to provide a balance between the rights of lawyers and prosecutors. The authority of the previously all-powerful prosecutors will be curbed; their power to issue arrest and search warrants has been transferred to the courts, and they will now have to prove their cases with hard evidence or face acquittals by skeptical juries. In criminal cases, the participation of defense lawyers will be mandatory, although they will still need the approval of prosecutors to call witnesses. Defendants will be able to admit guilt and avoid a trial.

These reforms have been welcomed by Russian liberals and

94

legal experts, but it remains to be seen how, and to what extent, they will be implemented in the coming years. In any event, most experts believe that the development of truly strong and respected courts in Russia will take decades, not years.

Nevertheless, more than fifty international law firms have opened offices in Moscow, and they appear to function remarkably well in representing the interests of their clients, both foreign and Russian. The problem, as many of the foreign law firms point out, is not too little law in Russia but too much, reflecting the highly regulated character of Soviet society that the new Russia has inherited.

Establishing a new company can take months and involves registering with several local and national government bodies. Foreign law firms are generally satisfied, however, with the progress made in judicial reform over the past ten years. As London's *Financial Times* has reported, one British law firm went to court in Moscow against a company closely linked to the FSB (the former KGB) and won. "Partly as a result of such cases," wrote the *Times*,

> the high commercial court in Moscow has a relatively good reputation for fairness. While the system is open to pressures—which some claim are getting worse as the current government looks to boost revenues—foreign investors appear generally happy with the protection they receive. They say Russia is different from some parts of Asia, where being foreign means you will probably lose. (Marsland 2001)

Echoing that idea, Alexandra Nesterenko, head of legal affairs in Moscow for Unilever, the Anglo-Dutch consumer products company, says she does not feel the company's foreign ownership has ever made a difference in Russian courts, although, she adds, "You can win a case and get the judgment but you cannot guarantee that you will get enforcement as a result" (in Marsland).

Order and Disorder

[Russia]...this most anarchic of nations.
—Francine du Plessix Gray, *Soviet Women*

Germans are known for *Ordnung* (order), and Russians for *nyeporyadok* (disorder). Yet order and disorder coexist in Russia, a fact of life to which visitors from the West will have to reconcile themselves.

In Russian literature it is Germans who demonstrate order, discipline, and efficiency. The classic example is Stolz, in Ivan Goncharov's novel *Oblomov*. Stolz is a model man of action, while Oblomov, his Russian opposite and friend, is a man of inaction who spends the first fifty pages of the novel getting out of bed in the morning. Oblomov is a favorite character of Russians, who see something of themselves in his inaction and disorder. It was not by chance that many high officials, diplomats, and military officers of Tsarist Russia were ethnic Germans from Russia's Baltic territories. Indeed, Russia's hard-working and businesslike President Putin has been described as "A German in the Kremlin" (Rahr 2000).

The Russian desire for order arises from her rulers' need to bring a measure of discipline to an unruly people and to marshal their productive potential for the security and well-being of state and society. Disorder derives from the anarchic strain in Russians, their rebellion against regimentation, defiance of authority, flouting of regulations when they believe they can safely do so, and disinclination to plan ahead.

Russians may respect authority, but they are not intimidated by it. Seeing themselves as coequal with others, they are not shy about speaking up in public or asserting themselves. Nor are they hesitant about forcefully requesting things that they believe are rightly theirs or that they would like to possess. Persistent and tenacious, they rarely accept no for an answer.

Westerners who arrive at Moscow's Sheremetyevo Airport— built by Germans—are struck by the confusion, in contrast to the efficiency of West European airports. By Soviet standards, however, Sheremetyevo is well run because it is a gateway to the country and was built to serve foreign travelers. The further one travels from Moscow, the greater the airport confusion.

One winter night in 1988, I changed planes in Sverdlovsk (now Yekaterinburg), a Siberian city on the eastern slope of the Ural Mountains. The third largest city in Russia and Yeltsin's hometown and former fiefdom, Sverdlovsk was closed to foreigners at the time. In fact, I must have been one of the first Americans in Sverdlovsk since U-2 pilot Gary Powers unexpectedly deplaned there in 1960. A major industrial center with a regional population of more than three million, Sverdlovsk had no Intourist facilities and no services for foreign travelers. (Sverdlovsk was not officially opened to foreigners until 1991.)

The Sverdlovsk air terminal recalled scenes of New York's Grand Central Station during rush hour. A huge crowd jammed the concourse. The public address system was barely intelligible. There were no seats and no places to rest except the rest rooms, which also had no seats.

When my flight was called, late as usual, there was the familiar pushing and shoving at the flight gate, not unlike a rugby scrum. After passengers were finally corralled into a small holding area and left standing, jammed together like sardines, there were more unexplained delays. When a bus eventually delivered us to the plane's ramp, we were left to wait another half hour in the frigid Siberian night while the plane was being readied. Between the flight gate and the plane ramp, tickets and identity documents of all passengers had been checked three times. Control was the primary concern of the airport officials, as it has been of all Russian governments.

Russian governments have traditionally had two main tasks, writes Berkeley's Martin Malia—to maintain order internally and to wage war externally (1961, 7). Maintaining internal order meant keeping the peasants in line, since they were some 90 percent of the population. Both tsars and commissars believed that without a strong hand to guide them, the unruly Russians would quickly descend into anarchy.

Communism strove to overcome Russian disorder by introducing rationalism and by planning and regimentation. "Try to understand the regimented way in which we live," a Russian teacher explained to me. "Things here are either yes or no, with no shades of interpretation in between."

There are regulations for everything. Uniformed *militsia* are seen everywhere in the cities, controlling pedestrian as well as motor vehicle traffic and enforcing regulations that often don't make sense. Jaywalking is strictly forbidden, and violators risk being cited by the militsia. Ronald Hingley relates how beach-masters at Black Sea resorts would blow whistles to command sunbathers to turn over at intervals so as to avoid sunburn (a command ignored by the sun-loving Russians) (1977, 207).

What should a foreign visitor do when stopped by the militsia for some minor infringement? My recommendation is to keep talking without raising your voice, admit to your transgression if you are clearly in the wrong—confession may bring forgive-ness—but also explain any extenuating circumstances. You can't beat city hall, in Russia as in the West, but the militsia can have a heart if appealed to on a personal level, if their authority is not questioned, and if slipped a little something on the side.

Russians drive on the right side of the road, but motor ve-hicles are not allowed to make left turns unless there is a traffic light with a green arrow. To turn left, drivers must proceed to a designated point where a *razvorot* (U-turn) may be made (very cautiously). It is only two blocks from Spaso House, the American ambassador's residence in Moscow, to the Ministry of Foreign Affairs, but to get there by car, the ambassador must drive more than a mile and make two U-turns along a circuitous route.

Returning to Moscow once with my family by rail from the West, I purchased a basket of food in Vienna to sustain us over the thirty-six-hour journey, because there was no dining car on the Soviet leg of the route. At Brest, the Polish-Soviet border crossing, a diligent Russian agricultural inspector rummaged through our food basket. Spying the bananas, she warned that they could not be brought into the country. (Whether this was to protect the local banana crop was not made clear.) "What to do?" I asked. "Eat them," she replied. So my children ate the bananas and brought the peels into Russia without objection.

Order is also valued because Russians believe it helps to provide a clear view of the future and thus avoids the uncertainty of the present that they so dislike. Communism played on this fear of the unknown by promising everything for the future but failing to deliver. That penchant for predicting the future and revising the past—rewriting the history books—has given rise to many jokes. According to one anekdot, Russians know the future, it's the past they are not sure of.

Despite the many regulations and the many officials to enforce them, Russia appears disorderly to the Westerner. As the Marquis de Custine saw it in 1839, "Every thing is here done by fits and starts, or with exceptions—a capricious system, which too often accords with the irregulated minds of the people..." (1989, 496). Eighty-five years later, Lenin expressed a similar view:

> It is simply the usual Russian intellectual inability to do practical things—inefficiency and lackadaisicalness. First they bustle around, do something, and then think about it, and when nothing comes of it, they run to complain...and want the matter brought up before the Political Bureau. (1943, 356)

Waste is widespread. In 1990, forty million tons of grain were lost at harvest time, roughly equal to the amount of grain the Soviet Union had to import from the West in that year (*The New York Times*, 20 August 1990). Spills of crude oil, Russia's largest foreign-currency earner, are estimated at 10–18 percent of total annual output (*Washington Post*, 28 October 1994). Grandiose projects are begun and left unfinished. Wherever people congregate, there is an aura of disarray.

"Russia's chronic chaos," writes Serge Schmemann in *The New York Times*, "is both its burden and its strength. Few nations could have endured what Russia has gone through in the last decade without a total breakdown" (20 February 1994).

But despite their manifest disorder, Russians appreciate the need for order, and many of them who visit the United States are confused by what they regard as the disorder of America. How can there be such abundance without a plan, central control, and a strong leader? How can there be national direction and unity of purpose with so many political views, religions, and discordant voices? And how can democracy, seen by many Russians as itself a manifestation of disorder, result in such strength and material abundance?

"In the United States," writes Rachel Connell, a Wellesley College student who spent a year in Russia, "when you follow the directions carefully…nine times out of ten things will work out as planned…." In Russia, she continues, "people are suspicious of something they receive without a hassle" (1991, 2).

School Days, Rule Days

> The Soviet school encouraged conformity and political docility, and generally suppressed initiative as well as independent thought.
> —Ben Eklof and Edward Dneprov
> *Democracy in the Russian School*

All of us have been formed by the schools we have attended, but Russians even more so. Many of the Russian characteristics described in earlier chapters have been reinforced by the schools Russians attended when they were young and by the Soviet system of education. It is therefore to the Soviet schools of the past that we must look in order to better understand the adult Russians whom we will be encountering today.

"Authorities in the Soviet state understood very well," wrote Canadian child education specialist Landon Pearson, "that the school is the most important social institution that exists outside the family for shaping the social and moral development of children" (1990, 94). To ensure that children would be shaped according to the needs of the Communist Party, Soviet education was marked by excessive centralization and close control by Moscow. The system was characterized, as Indiana University professor Ben Eklof describes it, by

> authoritarian approaches, uniforms, homework, rote learning in large classrooms, and a uniform and tightly controlled curriculum.... Funding was rigidly controlled by the central authorities, and directors of schools were left virtually no discretion in allocating revenues. (in Eklof and Dneprov 1993, 3–4)

Schools of the Soviet era had roots in the Russian past. Russian schools traditionally have been more than places to learn reading, writing, and 'rithmetic; they have also been tasked with moral education, the character building that Russians call *vospitaniye* (upbringing). Schools were to teach children how to behave and relate to others in society, a Russian version of civic education.

Another Russian tradition, in force since the nineteenth century, was uniform curricula and textbooks, in an effort to homogenize its far-flung imperium. As Pearson illustrated,

> It used to be possible...for a youngster to close his geography book in Moscow one morning, fly the long distance to Novosibirsk that afternoon for an extended visit to his grandfather, go to school next day, and find his new class studying the same page he had left the day before. (1990, 93)

Higher education was little different, explained former Minister of Education Yevgeny Tkachenko in the *Washington Post*.

> I spent my whole life in higher education. We...were not allowed to change not only the sequence of courses, but even to reduce by one hour the time allocated to some subject. We lived in the tight Procrustean bed of study plans stipulated for us by the Central Committee of the Party, and we were not allowed to deviate even by a single step to the right or to the left. (18 September 1995)

Other heritages of the Russian past included authoritarian methods, large classes, a preference for the spoken form of communication, oral over written exams, and rote learning.

Soviet education continued those traditions and added a few more. An extensive system of public schools blanketed the country, eliminated illiteracy, and raised the general level of learning among the populace. Vospitaniye continued in the schools but was manipulated to encourage conformity and serve the needs of the state. Indoctrination of political and social values began in kindergarten and continued through the school years in an effort to form a new "Soviet person" better able to contribute to the building of socialism.

The Soviet theory of education originated in the 1930s with Anton Makarenko, an influential but controversial educator who had worked for many years to rehabilitate and educate the homeless, delinquents, and juveniles. "Makarenko's theory became the official theory of Soviet education," wrote historians Mikhail Heller and Aleksandr Nekrich. "The child should be educated as a member of a collective organized along semimilitary lines and should be instilled with respect for the authority of the collective and of the person chosen to lead it" (1986, 286). From their earliest years, pupils were taught to think and act collectively, respect the authority of the teacher, and observe the rules of the classroom. (In Russian, the word *uchenik* [pupil] is used for primary and secondary schools; *student*, as elsewhere in Europe, is reserved for those in higher education.)

"A respectful and, indeed, slightly fearful attitude to adult authority," wrote Pearson, "is inculcated into Soviet children from the moment they set foot into an educational establishment. The degree of respect (and fear) increases with the age and status of the older person" (1990, 111–12).

Discipline was strict, and there was little or no discussion in the classroom. For each question by the teacher, there was one correct answer, and pupils soon learned that knowing the "right" answer would ensure good grades, which in turn would lead to admission to a university, a good job, and the perks that the state offered its educated elite. There were no electives, and teachers taught the required curriculum with little concern for the individual needs of pupils.

In the first year of school, pupils joined the Octobrists, their first collective, where as a group they performed socially useful activities such as participating in classroom cleanup, critiquing their classmates' attitudes toward learning, and listening to lectures on Lenin and the Soviet Motherland. In the third year they became Young Pioneers, and the level of group activity and political indoctrination increased. At age fourteen, most joined the *Komsomol* (Young Communist League), the prelude to Party membership. Peer pressure to join, as well as penalties for failure to do so, often proved difficult to resist. After 1985 the popularity of these organizations declined, and they were disbanded in 1991.

Economic demands also shaped education but left it at the mercy of two conflicting needs of the state. An expanding economy required workers who were better educated, which called for more years of schooling. But, as the Russian economy expanded, productivity also declined, and so more workers were needed, which required reducing the time students spent in school and moving them more rapidly into the workforce. The result was a back-and-forth of policy changes and reforms between general education, which prepared for entrance to institutions of higher education, and general education combined with vocational training, which produced the labor force.

The system was essentially two-track. Some pupils completed ten years of general education and went on to higher schools. Others ended their general education after eight years and transferred to (1) vocational schools that trained future workers and paraprofessionals or (2) specialized secondary schools that prepared graduates for skilled occupations as well as for higher education in industrial fields. Education was compulsory, free of charge, and coeducational. Schooling began at age seven and continued for ten years, four to six hours a day, five or six days a week. The conflict between general education and vocational training was temporarily resolved when another school year was added, nudging the total up to eleven, but that was done by starting school one year earlier, at age six. And in a concession to advocates of vocational training, pupils in all schools were required to learn a trade that would qualify them for employment.

By the end of the 1990s, however, changes had been made as a reform movement pushed slowly ahead, and control of the schools, as well as financial responsibility for them, was transferred to local authorities. Curricula have been revised, new textbooks written, the education system decentralized, local initiative in education encouraged, and private schools permitted. The once-obligatory school uniforms have been abolished, and political propaganda has been removed from the classroom and replaced by a more democratic and humane environment. Some electives have been added, and Saturday classes have been discontinued in many districts.

The decentralization of schools during the 1990s has given teachers the freedom to try out their own teaching techniques, especially in the new private schools that have proliferated. Change is coming to Russian schools, albeit slowly, and they will be different from those of the Soviet era that all of today's adults have attended.

Military training, which had been removed from the curriculum in 1991, was reinstated in 2000. Under a decree issued by President Putin, schoolboys age fifteen and older are now given premilitary training to prepare them for service in the armed forces. Schoolgirls, in a resumption of traditional Russian gender roles, are taught basic medical techniques for helping soldiers wounded in battle.

But many obstacles to reform remain. In addition to resistance by an entrenched bureaucracy, schools have not been adequately funded, and there are shortages of textbooks and teachers. Teachers have been poorly paid, their morale is low, and local authorities have not always had the funds to provide the necessary resources that teachers need.

Today, four years of primary education are followed by five of "incomplete" secondary education. After these nine years, about half of all pupils complete two more years of general secondary education in preparation for higher education. The others transfer to either vocational schools or specialized secondary schools. Parental pressure, however, has increased the demand for higher education and its rewards, and since the 1970s it has also been possible for graduates of vocational schools to advance to higher education. In addition, plans have been announced to add another year of schooling by 2007, for a total of twelve.

For the gifted and talented there are state schools specializing in math, science, and the arts. Other schools specialize in foreign languages, producing graduates who are nearly bilingual.

With no formal division between primary school, "incomplete" secondary, and secondary school, pupils in the general education track remain in the same building with the same classmates, often in the same homeroom, throughout all eleven years of school, forging strong bonds of friendship that last throughout life. Many of the friends and familiar faces with whom Russians feel so comfortable and secure are based on those old school ties.

Applicants to institutions of higher learning take oral and written exams at the end of the ninth and eleventh years as well as entrance exams given by higher-education institutions. Some 20 percent of those aged eighteen to twenty-one are enrolled in colleges and universities, but that figure includes many who are enrolled in evening or extension courses rather than studying full-time.

Competition for entrance to elite institutions is very keen, and nepotism, influence, and bribery are widespread. There is, however, no gender discrimination in admissions, and the number of male and female students is about equal. Women, however, predominate in the humanities, medicine, and education, a result more of traditional Russian notions of "female occupations" than of overt discrimination.

Getting good grades in school and being admitted to higher education are important for young men as a way of avoiding or postponing military service, which is mandatory at the age of eighteen. University students are automatically given a defer‑ment, thereby avoiding military service with its hazing, humili‑ation, and degradation.

Higher‑education institutions each year reserve a number of places for so‑called "commercial students," who may not have the high grades necessary for admission but are able to pay a substantial tuition fee. As a result, students with lower grades who can pay are admitted, while students with good grades but who cannot pay the higher fee may be denied admittance and be required instead to serve in the military.

To correct that inequity, plans have been made to introduce a new unified state exam in summer 2004 so that admission to higher education will be based solely on academic results rather than ability to pay. The new exam, similar to the German Abitur, French Baccalaureate, British General Certificate of Secondary Education (GCSE), and American Scholastic Aptitude Test (SAT), will replace both the *vypustnoi examen* (graduating exam) of Russian secondary schools and the admission exams offered by universities.

The broad liberal arts education leading to a bachelor's de‑gree, customary in the United Kingdom and the United States, is unknown in Russia. Rather, higher education is narrowly specialized to produce graduates in professions needed by the economy. On applying to a university or other higher school, students must choose their major field of study, and that choice may well determine whether they are accepted. For decades, a quota for the number of first‑year students in each field of study was set by the future needs of the economy as determined by the five‑year economic plans. For example, the projected need for petroleum engineers five years hence would determine the number of students allowed to enter the five‑year study program in petroleum engineering. That practice, however, has been mod‑erated in recent years, and higher‑education institutions now have increased flexibility in determining their enrollments.

First‑year students are formed into *gruppy* (groups) within each department. With few electives, students remain in those groups, with the same classmates, through their undergraduate years, a continuation of the group bonding that began in primary school. The length of study for future teachers with one specialization is four years, but most take a fifth year and specialize in two disciplines. Most other students also study for five years, earning the degree of certified specialist. Medical doctors study six years, followed by an internship and residency. The transition to the Western system is under way, however, and students will be able to earn a bachelor's degree after four years and a master's after an additional two years.

Graduate study, the *aspirantura*, is three years and leads to the *kandidat nauk* (candidate of sciences) degree, somewhat short of a Western doctorate. Full professors usually have the full doctorate, considered higher than a Western Ph.D. and awarded after additional research.

Instruction is largely theoretical and highly specialized. Students attend lectures and take notes but rarely challenge their professors. Russian students excel in mathematics and science, but the system generally does not produce well-rounded graduates who are able to respond to the challenges of technological change they will face in the workplace. Russian universities, moreover, emphasize teaching. Research, for the most part, is the preserve of the various academies of science, which also award academic degrees. The separation of teaching and research is a shortcoming of Russian higher education and a recognized handicap for both students and professors.

Respect for teachers and professors continues. Some university professors still expect their students to rise when the professor enters the classroom, and a student will address a professor by his or her first name and patronymic, but never by the first name alone.

Russian educators who have visited Western schools have been impressed by the sophisticated equipment, the libraries, and the laboratories. But they have also noted with approval the interaction between students and teachers, the encouragement of independent thinking rather than rote learning, the wide choice of electives and independent study, the students' self-reliance, and the responsibility they assume for their own education.

Russian education, however, does have its strengths. Russian immigrants in the United States have learned that their children are two to three years ahead of American students in math and science, and they are also more knowledgeable about literature and history. This is due largely to their Russian teachers who, although poorly paid, were well prepared and dedicated.

5

Personal Encounters

Russians are more emotional, more likely to strike deep friendships, less superficially gregarious. They make great sacrifices for those within their trusted circle, and they expect real sacrifices in return. Their willingness, indeed their eagerness, to engage at a personal level makes private life in Russia both enormously rich and incredibly entangling. Close emotional bonds are part of Russia's enchantment and also its complexity.

—Hedrick Smith, *The New Russians*

The City

The city itself in Russia is an implanted thing, and…the urban man who has created the civilizations of the West is still in the making here. His habitual loneliness, his totally private life, his ignorance of his neighbors, his go-it-alone psychology—these are still in conflict in Russia with an older way of communal existence.

—Inge Morath and Arthur Miller, *In Russia*

First-time visitors to Russia will be struck—literally as well as figuratively—by the large crowds of people they encounter and the ever present body contact. Russian cities swarm with people. Forced industrialization moved masses of peasants from the warm and personal environment of their native villages to the cold and impersonal surroundings of large cities. Between 1926 and

1939, the Moscow and Leningrad regions grew by 3,500,000 each (Stites 1989, 244).

There is no real analogy in the United States (or other countries), as Inge Morath and Arthur Miller point out, although Americans can look back to something similar in their own cities in the days before World War I

> when the cities were filling up with country people who had to learn to be up-to-date—to forget the ideas of mutual help...and to relate themselves to an impersonal administration rather than to officials they knew and to personalities they understood and who understood them. (1969, 15)

Most urban residents in Russia are only one, two, or three generations removed from their ancestral villages and peasant traditions. As Ronald Hingley describes them, "...even in the towns—in Moscow or Tula, say—a Russian crowd seems to react in a more peasant-like manner, however defined, than would be the case in Rome, Munich, or Pittsburgh" (1977, 179). The cities became "ruralized," writes Richard Stites, "...imbued with peasant values—at home, on the streets, and at work. Urban civilization did not efface rural mentalities; rather, the opposite occurred" (1989, 244–45). Residents of St. Petersburg, however, will argue that people are more polite in "Piter," as their more European city is affectionately called.

Despite the dislocations derived from their move from village to city, Russians regard urban life as infinitely better than rural. In the city there are new opportunities not only for work but also for education, culture, and recreation. Housing and municipal services, however, have not kept pace with the large influx of new residents.

Most city dwellers live in small apartments in large multistoried buildings rather than in detached houses. But because of the continuing housing shortage as well as a real estate boom resulting from the privatization of apartments, many Russians still live in a *kommunalka* (communal apartment)—one family

occupying one or two rooms and sharing a kitchen and bath-
room with one or more other families. The need to find relief
from indoor crowding is one reason why so many Russians are
seen on the streets.

Stores and markets these days are full of food and consumer
goods—albeit at prices many cannot afford—and Russians no
longer need to stand in long lines to make their essential purchases. In some of the older stores, however, customers may
still have to stand in line three times to make a purchase—first
to learn what is for sale and how much it costs, then to pay a
cashier, and finally to present the cash receipt to a salesperson
and pick up the purchase.

Unmet demands can make Russians very aggressive about trying to acquire things they need or want but cannot afford, and
they are not at all bashful about making such requests to foreign
visitors, who may be put off by their persistence. A first response
of no is never accepted as final. Believing that every response can
be manipulated and changed, Russians will repeat their requests
over and over again, adding a new twist each time.

Requests may be for medicines not available, scholarships to
foreign universities, books or laboratory equipment required for
research, or assistance in emigrating. Visitors will need to be
patient in rebuffing requests that they cannot or do not wish to
fulfill. They should also not make promises they cannot keep or
agree to miracles they cannot perform.

One type of request which visitors can easily fulfill is helping Russians establish contact with professional counterparts
abroad. Russians will seek names and addresses of persons or
organizations in their profession or in fields in which they have
a personal interest. The intent is to establish contact and exchange information with the outside world, which was difficult
to do in the Soviet era.

Others may seek help locating relatives abroad. One Russian
I met in the middle of Siberia, whose Texas-born father had
emigrated to the Soviet Union during the Depression, had been
trying for years, without success, through both U.S. and Soviet

government channels, to find his long-lost American relatives. On my return home, I was able to find several of his family members, who had been trying for years to locate their Russian cousin. For that Russian, I was indeed a miracle maker.

Large crowds make municipal authorities apprehensive, and their response is crowd control. Uniformed militsia (*police* was considered a capitalist term), are ever present in Russian cities. At sports events and other activities that attract large crowds, long convoys of militsia trucks may be parked nearby in case a crowd gets unruly or out of control, as occasionally occurs. In 1982, at a soccer match in Moscow's Luzhniki Stadium, according to *The New York Times*, some 340 fans were crushed to death by a surging crowd (19 July 1989). And more than 500 people were suffocated or trampled to death on Moscow streets in 1953, when Joseph Stalin's body lay in state (Heller and Nekrich 1986, 508). It is prudent to stay on the fringes of large crowds to avoid being swept away and trampled.

Russians do not always queue up naturally, as do West Europeans and Americans. Rather than line up and patiently await their turn, Russians will at times storm buildings and box offices—pushing, shoving, and elbowing—determined to gain access or obtain their share before whatever they seek is gone. At airports, even when all passengers are ticketed and have reservations, Russians will throng around the flight gate and plane ramp, anxious lest they not be boarded.

At popular concerts and sports events, persons without tickets have been known to storm the gate in an attempt to gain admission. Such storming is done not only by the *narod* (common people) but also by the intelligentsia. I witnessed one such Sturm und Drang in 1969 when music students stormed the entrance to the Moscow Conservatory Great Hall, seeking admission to a performance of Bach's *Passion According to St. John* by a visiting West German ensemble. Bach was rarely performed in Russia at that time, and the hall had been sold out in advance to music lovers with connections.

Friends and Familiar Faces

Better to have one hundred friends than one hundred rubles.
—Russian proverb

The value of the ruble varies but not the value of friends. Friends and familiar faces are the key to getting things done in Russia, and foreigners who cultivate close relationships will have a big advantage in doing business with Russians.

Sol Hurok, the legendary American impresario who pioneered North American tours by Soviet dance and music groups, would visit the Soviet Union periodically to audition performing artists and to select those he would sign for performances abroad. Traveling alone, Hurok would negotiate and sign contracts for extensive U.S. coast-to-coast tours by such large ensembles as the Bolshoi Ballet and Moscow Philharmonic.

On one such trip in 1969, when Hurok was eighty years old, I asked him how he could sign contracts for such large and costly undertakings without lawyers and others to advise him. "I have been coming here for many years and doing business with the Russians," he replied confidently. "I simply write out a contract by hand on a piece of paper, and we both sign it. They know and trust me."

A similar but more recent experience is reported by William McCulloch, an American whose business activities in Russia include housing construction and telecommunications. The key to doing business in Russia, says McCulloch, is finding the right partner—one with whom a basis of trust is established over time. "You cannot bring in an army of New York lawyers and have an ironclad deal. You have to have a clear understanding with the right partner about what you are doing." Such an understanding, he adds, makes it possible to negotiate one's way through the Russian political, economic, and banking systems (1994).

A different experience is reported by an American who met with a group of people from various parts of Russia to help form a national coalition in support of democracy. Assembled in the room were people with a common purpose and a shared commitment to democracy. Yet, in their first meeting it became apparent that their loyalties were to their local organizations, each with its own parochial interests, and not to the broad coalition and platform they hoped to forge. Suspicious of each other, they were reluctant to speak up in public. They also did not trust the interpreter, a Russian whom the American had brought with him. Many more meetings were required before the American—talking with the participants individually and in small groups and eating, drinking, and socializing with them—was able to overcome their initial distrust, not only of him but of their fellow Russians, and eventually help them to forge a viable coalition.

Russians rely on a close network of family, friends, and co-workers as protection against the risks and unpredictability of daily life. In the village commune, Russians felt safe and secure in the company of family and neighbors. Today, in the city, they continue to value familiar faces and mistrust those they do not know.

Visitors who know a Russian from a previous encounter will have a big advantage. First-time travelers to Russia are advised to ask friends who already know the individuals they will be meeting to put in a good word for them in advance of their visits. And ideally the same traveler should return for subsequent visits and not be replaced by someone else from his or her firm or organization.

Despite its vast size, Russia is run on the basis of personal connections. In the workplace and private life, Russians depend on those they know—friends who owe them favors, former classmates, fellow military veterans, and others whom they trust. The bureaucracy is not expected to respond equitably to a citizen's request. Instead, Russians will call friends and ask for their help.

The friendship network also extends to the business world. Business managers, short of essential parts or materials, will use their personal contacts to obtain the necessary items. Provide a spare part or commodity for someone, and receive something in return. Without such contacts, production would grind to a halt.

Westerners who want something from their government will approach the responsible official, state their case, and assume (or hope) that law and logic will prevail. Russians in the same situation, mistrustful of the state and its laws, will approach friends and acquaintances and ask them to put in a good word with the official who will decide.

The process is reciprocal; those who do favors for Russians can expect favors in return. I once offered some friendly advice to a newly arrived Soviet cultural attaché in Washington on how to get things done in the United States. He returned the favor many times over, smoothing my way through the Moscow bureaucratic maze as we developed a mutually advantageous pro-fessional relationship. I was pleased to consider him a friend.

The word *friend*, however, must be used carefully in Russia. For most Americans, anyone who is not an enemy seems to be a friend. An American can become acquainted with a com-plete stranger and in the next breath describe that person as a friend. American friendships, however, are compartmentalized, often centering around colleagues in an office, neighbors in a residential community, or participants in recreational activities. This reflects the American reluctance to get too deeply involved with the personal problems of others. A friend in need may be a friend indeed, but an American is more likely to refer a needy friend to a professional for help rather than become involved in the friend's personal troubles.

Not so with Russians, for whom friendship is all-encompassing and connotes a special relationship. Dancer Mikhail Baryshnikov, when asked about the difference between Russian and American friendships, replied,

> In Russia, because the society has been so closed, you're sharing your inside with your friends. Your views on society. Political points of view. It's a small circle of people whom you trust. And

you get so attached. Talking with friends becomes your second
nature. A need. Like, at four o'clock in the morning, without
a phone call, your friend can come to your house, and you're
up and putting the teapot on. That kind of friendship. (*Parade
Magazine*, 8 October 1989, 27)

The Russian language has different words for "friend" (*drug*,
pronounced "droog") and "acquaintance" (*znakomy*), and these
words should not be misused. A drug is more like a "bosom
buddy," someone to trust, confide in, and treat like a member
of the family. Such friendships are not made easily or quickly.
It takes time to develop, but when it is made and nurtured, a
Russian friendship will embrace the entire person. Russians will
ask friends for time and favors that many Westerners would
regard as impositions.

Friendship with a Russian is not to be treated lightly. One
visitor describes it as smothering, and some will find that it is
more than they can handle. As one Russian explained, "Between
Russian friends, what's theirs is yours and what's yours is theirs,
especially if it's in the refrigerator."

Americans tend to be informal in their speech—candid, direct,
and without the rituals, polite forms, and the indirect language
common to many other cultures. Russians welcome and appreciate such informal talk but usually only after a certain stage in
the relationship has been reached.

Addressing an American or Briton presents a dilemma for
Russians. Their language has equivalents for "Mr." (*Gospodin*)
and "Mrs." (*Gospozha*), but until recently these were considered
relics of the prerevolutionary past and were not in common use.
Now, with the demise of communism, Russians may use these
older terms of address in formal meetings.

The preferred form of address among Russians, however, and
the one most likely to be used in the initial stage of a relationship, is the first name and patronymic (father's first name plus
an affix). For example, a man named Boris, whose father was
Nikolai, is addressed as Boris Nikolayevich (Boris, son of Nikolai). Similarly, a woman named Mariya whose father was Fyodor

(Theodore), would be Mariya Fyodorovna (with the feminine ending *-a*). Use of the patronymic does not signify friendship but is less formal than "Mr." or "Ms."

With the friendship stage comes use of the first name by itself, or a nickname. But first-name usage with a foreigner does not necessarily indicate that the friendship stage has been reached, as it would with another Russian. It does signify, however, the next stage in a developing relationship.

Like most European languages, Russian has two forms of *you*. The more formal *vy* is used between strangers and acquaintances and in addressing people of higher position. The informal *ty*, akin to the old English *thou* and the French *tu* or German *du*, is reserved for friends, family members, and children and is also used in talking down to someone and in addressing animals. Readers will surely appreciate the need for care in using the familiar form.

Which of these forms should foreigners use in addressing Russians? That will depend on the state of the relationship, and it may differ in each case. When in doubt, let the Russians decide, and follow their lead.

Carry a good supply of business cards (*vizitnaya*, in Russian, from "visiting cards"). Have them printed in English on one side and Russian (in Cyrillic) on the other. Be sure to include your title, academic degrees, and anything else that might impress.

At Home

At home do as you wish, but in public as you are told.
—Russian proverb

Russians live two separate and distinct lives—one at work and the other at home. At work, they can be brusque and discourteous and will watch what they say. At home, within the intimate circle of family and friends, they feel secure and are relaxed, warm, and hospitable. They are sharing and caring, and they speak their own minds.

As Morath and Miller describe it,

> There is still a homeliness about many Russians that has the scent
> of the country in it, a capacity for welcoming strangers with open,
> unabashed curiosity, a willingness to show feeling, and above all
> a carelessness about the passing of time. (1969, 15)

When asked what Russians were thinking during the many
decades of political repression, legal scholar Nina Belyaeva
explained,

> People did not connect themselves with the power of the state.
> On the one hand, they seemed from outside not to care, so they
> seemed submissive. But inside, they said, "Inside, I am me. They
> can't touch me. When I'm in my kitchen with my friends, I am
> free." (in Geyer 1990)

The kitchen is indeed the center of social life, and visitors
should not pass up opportunities to get into those kitchens and
see Russians at home. There is no better way to get to know
Russians than over food and drink or merely sitting around a
kitchen table sipping tea. And when hosting Russians in your
own home, bear in mind that Russians will appreciate dining in
the kitchen, which gives them the feeling they are being treated
as family rather than as guests in a formal dining room.

"The secret of social life in Russia," says Stites, "is conviviality
around a table, drinking, telling jokes, laughing. When you get
to that point, the battle is half won" (1991).

Hospitality is spontaneous and intrinsic to the culture. Russians will share what they have and make their guests feel at
home. Dinner may be served in the kitchen or in a parlor that
doubles as a bedroom. The dishes may not match, and the table
service will be informal, but the visitor will be made to feel
welcome. Food will be tasty, and guests will wonder how the
hosts could afford the many delicacies. As in most European
countries, the hot meal is usually taken in the middle of the
day—the legacy of an agricultural society where sustenance was

needed for work in the fields—and the evening meal is more like a supper. Today, however, the old rules no longer apply, and the big meal may be offered in the early afternoon or in the evening. A meal always begins with wishing others at the table *priyatnovo appetita*, an equivalent of the French *bon appétit*.

Friends and relatives may drop in unexpectedly and join the table. Spirits will flow, and the talk will be lively and natural. Conversation is a very important part of social life, and over food and drink Russians open up and reveal their innermost thoughts.

Describing conversations with Russians, Geoffrey Hosking writes, "The exchange and exploration of ideas proceeds [sic] with utter spontaneity and at the same time concentration. In my experience, the art of conversation is pursued in Moscow at a higher level than anywhere else in the world" (1990, 13).

Guests should observe an old custom and bring a gift. Be cautious, however, about expressing admiration for an object in a Russian home. In a spontaneous gesture of hospitality, the host may present the admired object to the guest, and the offer will be difficult to refuse.

Russians welcome inquiries about family and children, and they will be interested in learning about a visitor's family. Such interest is genuine and should not be seen as merely making small talk. The fastest way to a Russian host's heart is to speak frankly about personal matters—joys and sorrows, successes and failures—which show that you are a warm human being and not just another cold Westerner.

Family and children are important in Russian life, although society's current ills—inadequate housing, lack of privacy, crime, alcoholism, and divorce—have taken their toll. In cities, families with one child are the norm, and I was always surprised when Russians expressed admiration on learning that I was the father of three.

How visitors live is also of great interest. Bring photos of family, home, and recreational activities, which will all be of interest. Russians are curious about the lifestyles of others in professions and occupations similar to their own, and they will not hesitate to inquire about a visitor's salary or the cost of a home and how many rooms it has. When a celebrated Soviet writer once visited my home in the Washington suburbs, I expected our talk to be about life and literature. Instead, the world-renowned author requested a tour of the house and was full of questions about the heating, air conditioning, and insulation, how much everything cost, and whether the house was my year-round home or my weekend dacha.

Handshaking is required practice for men, both on arrival and upon taking leave, with eye contact maintained during the handshake. Men do not shake hands with a woman unless she extends hers first, and women should not be surprised if their hands are kissed rather than shaken. Shaking hands over a threshold, however, is an omen of bad luck and should never be done. If you are a man, physical signs of affection toward your host (embracing or touching) are good, but show reserve toward his wife. She will not appreciate hugs and kisses but will welcome flowers—odd numbers only, though, but not thirteen. An even number of flowers is considered unlucky. Old superstitions survive.

Once over the threshold and into the home, you will likely encounter a cloud of smoke. The antismoking campaign has not yet reached Russia, where almost 70 percent of adults smoke; Russians are literally smoking themselves to death. In a small apartment or office with windows closed tight in winter, the smoke can be oppressive for nonsmokers.

Offer to remove your shoes, especially in winter or inclement weather. Russians do not wear street shoes at home. They may declare that it is not necessary for foreign visitors to remove their shoes but will appreciate it when they do, and will likely offer slippers.

Due to rising crime, Russians are triple- and quadruple-locking their apartment doors and are reluctant to open them without knowing who is standing outside. To be sure they know who you are, call beforehand from a nearby public phone and tell them you will be there shortly.

Puzzling for Westerners is the Russian passion for *morozhenoye* (ice cream), which they consume outdoors even in the dead of winter with the temperature below freezing. Russian ice cream is very good, and the favorite flavor is vanilla.

A greater passion, of course, is tea, the favorite Russian non-alcoholic drink. On a per capita basis, Russia is second only to Great Britain in tea consumption. Approximately half of the Russian adults are believed to drink at least five cups a day. Russians like their tea black and loose, and tea bags are popular only with young businesspeople and students, for whom time is important. Traditionally, tea is brewed in a samovar (self-boiler), where the water is heated in a metal vessel with an inner cylinder filled with burning coals. Another novelty for foreign visitors may be the *podstakannik* (literally, an "underglass"), a metal glass holder with a handle on one side. If you are lucky enough to observe tea prepared and drunk in such a manner in someone's home, consider yourself fortunate.

The Toast

Za vashe zdorovye (To your health).

—short Russian toast

Visitors should be prepared to frequently raise their glasses in a toast. Toasting in Russia is serious business, and in the Republic of Georgia it is an art form.

Toasts are usually given at the beginning of a meal when vodka is drunk with the first course, or at the end of the meal with the sweet wine or champagne that is served with dessert, and often throughout the meal as well. Hosts toast first, and the ranking guest is expected to follow with a return toast. With each toast, guests clink glasses with those of other guests while looking at each guest directly and making eye contact. The person being toasted also drinks.

A toast in Russia is a short speech. For starters, there are the obligatory thanks to the hosts for their hospitality. This may be followed by references to the purpose of the visit, international cooperation, peace and friendship, and the better world we hope to leave to our children as a result of our cooperation.

When called on to make a toast, be poetic and dramatic, and let your "soul" show. Russians appreciate a show of emotion and imagination. Don't hesitate to exaggerate; make the most of your toast. Humor may be used, but the substance of the toast should be serious. Russians will judge a toast as an indication of the seriousness of a visitor's purpose. Prudent travelers will have a few toasts prepared in advance—they will surely be needed.

Women, by tradition, do not toast in Russia, but more and more Russian women are now doing so, and Russians will not be surprised if a foreign woman raises her glass and gives a toast. And if a hostess is present, she gets a separate toast, complimenting her on her home, food, and hospitality—but never on her looks, as pretty as she may be.

In Georgia, which is now independent, toasting is continuous throughout the meal, and a guest's glass is never left empty. Eating, drinking, and hospitality are a way of life in Georgia, a wine-producing country, and guests should be prepared for meals that last several hours. Once, when I was in Georgia as the leader of an American delegation, my hosts had the courtesy to ask in advance whether I preferred a three- or four-hour dinner. I opted for the three-hour "short" dinner, which actually lasted five hours—with continuous eating, drinking, animated conversation, music, singing, and endless toasting. *Omnia pro patria.*

Mir i druzhba (peace and friendship) is a toast—as well as a slogan—that visitors will often hear in Russia; so often, in fact, that it begins to sound more and more like the political catchphrase it once was throughout the communist world. Of the misuse of the word *peace*, Vaclav Havel, the Czech playwright who became his country's democratically elected president in 1990, has written,

> For forty years now I have read it on the front of every building and in every shop window in my country. For forty years, an

allergy to that beautiful word has been engendered in me as in every one of my fellow citizens because I know what the word has meant here for the past forty years: ever mightier armies ostensibly to defend peace. (1990, 8)

Political slogans aside, the Russian yearning for peace and friendship should not be seen as an attempt to delude the West but as a reflection of their traditional yearning for harmony, cooperation, and community. Russians have good reason to want peace and friendship with other countries, although that did not prevent their leaders from using armed force when they believed it necessary—in Hungary in 1956, Czechoslovakia in 1968, Afghanistan in 1979, and their own country as well.

World War II with its death and destruction is a part of every Russian's life, experienced either directly or through older family members. More than twenty million Soviet citizens died in the war, and much of European Russia was overrun by German armies before their advance was halted and reversed at Stalingrad. Leningrad was besieged for nine hundred days, and more than a million of its people died there of hunger alone, more than ten times the deaths at Hiroshima. The Great Patriotic War, as the Russians call it, was truly one of the epic events of Russian history, one that threatened the very existence of the state. More recently, another generation has known war, in Afghanistan and Chechnya.

Do Russians fear a war with the United States? Some of them may, because the U.S. is the only country with the military might to vanquish them. Russians, moreover, have a very high respect for American technology, military as well as civilian. When Russians toast "peace and friendship" with Americans, they really mean it.

Alcohol, the Other "Ism"

More people are drowned in a glass than in the ocean.
—Russian proverb

124

To all the other "isms" that help one to understand Russians, alcoholism must unfortunately be added. For Karl Marx, religion was the opiate of the people. For Russians, the opiate has been alcohol.

The Russian affinity for alcohol was described by the Marquis de Custine in 1839:

> The greatest pleasure of these people is drunkenness; in other words, forgetfulness. Unfortunate beings! they must dream, if they would be happy. As proof of the good temper of the Russians, when the mugics [*muzhiks*] get tipsy, these men, brutalized as they are, become softened, instead of infuriated. Unlike the drunkards of our country, who quarrel and fight, they weep and embrace each other. Curious and interesting nation! (1989, 137)

In our time, the distinguished Russian novelist and literary critic Andrei Sinyavsky has described drunkenness as

> our *idée fixe*. The Russian people drink not from need and not from grief, but from an age-old requirement for the miraculous and the extraordinary—drink, if you will mystically, striving to transport the soul beyond earth's gravity and return it to its sacred noncorporeal state. Vodka is the Russian muzhik's White Magic; he decidedly prefers it to Black Magic—the female. (1965, 1)

Per capita consumption of alcohol in Russia, Western Europe, and the United States is not very different. Americans, however, drink more wine and beer, Russians more hard liquor, mainly vodka. And like their north European neighbors, from Ireland to Finland, Russians drink their distilled spirits neat, without a mixer.

Vodka is described by Hedrick Smith as "one of the indispensable lubricants and escape mechanisms of Russian life.... Russians drink to blot out the tedium of life, to warm themselves from the chilling winters, and they eagerly embrace the escapism it offers" (1976, 120–21).

To take the measure of a man, Russians will want to drink with him, and the drinking will be serious. Foreign visitors should not attempt to match their hosts in drinking. This is one competition Russians should be allowed to win, as they inevitably will.

Vodka is also a prelude to business transactions. As one Western financier explains,

> Business is done differently everywhere. In Russia...any negotiation is preceded by an arranged dinner that is extremely boozy.... You can't expect to go in there with a stiff upper lip and a pressed suit. It's a test. The trick is to play the game, but not get distracted by it." (in Hunt 2001)

Vodka is drunk straight, ice-cold in small glasses in one "bottoms-up" gulp. At meals it is served with the *zakuski*, tasty Russian cold meats, fish, fresh and pickled vegetables, and caviar when affordable. Guests should bear in mind that the zakuski are only the first course and that several other courses will follow. With each round of vodka, there will be a toast, and the drinking and toasting will continue until the bottle—or bottles—are empty.

What should a visitor do when confronted with vodka and the obligatory toasts at a dinner where the visitor is guest of honor? If the guest knows when to stop, then by all means, drink and enjoy it. Guests who fear they will not know their limit can abstain, pleading doctor's orders or religious reasons. Or they can down their first drink and slowly nurse subsequent rounds through the evening.

Russians prefer to drink while seated, and the stand-up cocktail party, a Western innovation, is consequently alien. Anyone invited to a Russian home should expect to be seated, to be fed a substantial repast, and to drink during the meal. When invited to an American home, Russians will expect more than chips or cheese and crackers.

A night on the town usually consists of an evening with friends at a restaurant—eating, drinking, and dancing for several hours to very loud music. The eating will also be serious. Older Russians recall the difficult days when food was scarce, and they relish a good meal with many courses, one that can last several hours. Toward the end of the evening, there may be a bloody brawl among the more serious drinkers, which ends only when the militsia arrives.

"Demon vodka," as the Russians call it, is the national vice. Excessive vodka consumption is a major cause of absenteeism, low productivity, industrial accidents, road accidents, homicides and suicides, wife beating, divorce and other family problems, birth defects, and a declining longevity. Orphanages are full of children abandoned by alcoholic parents. The problem is intensified by the pervasiveness of low-quality and illegally produced alcohol. In 2001, some 47,000 Russians died of alcohol poisoning, while many more suffered from diseases caused or aggravated by alcohol.

With the economic, social, and physical ills that alcohol causes, it was not surprising that the first published decree when former President Mikhail Gorbachev took office in 1985 signaled a state campaign against it. The intent was to limit consumption, but the immediate result was a sugar shortage when Russians purchased more sugar to increase their production of home brew. Consumption of products with alcoholic content also increased—industrial alcohol, jet fuel, insecticide, perfume, shoe polish, and toothpaste—thus creating additional shortages. According to official Soviet sources, more than 10,000 citizens died from alcohol substitutes in 1987 and more than 11,000 in 1988 (Feshbach 1989, 12). And the toll has continued to rise; according to the Russian Ministry of Health, 27,000 deaths resulted from alcohol poisoning during the first ten months of 2001, as reported by the *Boston Globe* (3 November 2001). Gorbachev's anti-alcohol campaign also resulted in a 10 to 20 percent reduction in tax revenues (Goldman 1990, 38). An admitted failure, the program was scrapped after three years. The anti-alcohol campaign, however, did have one virtue. At the peak of the campaign, violent crime dropped, only to rise sharply when the campaign ended.

Alcohol continues to take its toll, contributing heavily to the increasing mortality rate for Russian males who imbibe toxic home brew (*samogon*) and alcohol-based substances. One down-on-the-farm favorite has been thick slabs of bread coated with tractor oil. Priyatnovo appetita! And travelers to Russia should beware of alcohol that is sold in street kiosks at bargain-basement prices. That bottle with the authentic-looking label may not be genuine, and it may be bad for your health.

A bill to impose criminal penalties on producers of home brew was introduced in the Duma in December 2001 but was defeated. Authors of the bill argued that action was needed because entire villages were addicted to alcohol. Opponents noted that half of all rural residents made moonshine and that giving new powers to law enforcement agencies could result in increased misuse of power.

Vodka is a basic ingredient of Russian life and will not be easily eliminated. During the height of the antialcohol campaign, I attended several official lunches where wine was the strongest drink served, but vodka bottles were passed under the table between the thirsty guests.

Vodka does have one virtue. While it can produce a hangover when drunk to excess, it seldom causes headache or nausea. And with zakuski, in moderation, it is the ideal drink.

Vranyo, *the Russian Fib*

> Yes, the Russian is incapable of telling downright lies; but seems equally incapable of telling the truth. The intermediate phenomenon for which he feels the utmost love and tenderness resembles neither truth nor *lozh* [lie]. It is *vranyo*. Like our native aspen, it pops up uninvited everywhere, choking other varieties; like the aspen it is no use for firewood or carpentry; and, again like the aspen, it is sometimes beautiful.
>
> —Leonid Andreyev, "Pan-Russian Vranyo"[*]

[*] For this quote, as well as other material on vranyo, I am indebted to Ronald Hingley, 1977, *The Russian Mind*, 91, and "That's No Lie, Comrade," *Problems of Communism* 11, no. 2 (1962): 47–55.

Russians can fudge the facts, a national characteristic called *vranyo* (with the accent on the second syllable). Dictionaries translate *vranyo* as "lies, fibs, nonsense, idle talk, twaddle," but like many Russian terms, it is really untranslatable. Americans might call it "tall talk" or "white lies," but "fib" perhaps comes closest because vranyo, as Russian writer Leonid Andreyev noted, is somewhere between the truth and a lie. Vranyo is indeed an art form, perhaps beautiful to Russians but annoying to Westerners and others who value the unvarnished truth.

In its most common form today, vranyo is an inability to face the facts, particularly when the facts do not reflect favorably on Russia. Tourist guides are masters of vranyo, as are Russians who represent their country abroad. When ideology or politics dictates a particular position, they are likely to evade, twist, or misstate facts in order to put the best possible spin on a potentially embarrassing situation. As Boris Fedorov, a former deputy prime minister of Russia has put it, "There are several layers of truth in Russia. Nothing is black or white, fortunately or unfortunately" (*Washington Post*, 1 May 2001).

Russians, however, do not consider vranyo to be dishonest, nor should foreign visitors. As Fyodor Dostoyevsky wrote,

> Among our Russian intellectual classes the very existence of a non-liar is an impossibility, the reason being that in Russia even honest men can lie.... I am convinced that in other nations, for the great majority, it is only scoundrels who lie; they lie for practical advantage, that is, with directly criminal aims. (in Hingley 1977, 105)

And, as Dostoyevsky might have put it, if vranyo is not a crime, it should not be punished.

When using vranyo, Russians know that they are fibbing and expect that their interlocutors will also know. But it is considered bad manners to directly challenge the fibber, although it can be done with tact. As Hingley advises, the victim of vranyo should "convey subtly, almost telepathically, that he is aware of what is going on, that he appreciates the performance and does not despise his...host simply because the conditions of the latter's office obliged him to put it on" (1962, 54).

That advice was once put to good use in Moscow when I was a victim of vranyo. At a lunch given by the American ambassador, all the Russian guests had arrived on time but one, and he had called me the day before to confirm his attendance. After waiting thirty minutes, the ambassador asked me to call our tardy guest and inquire whether we could expect him. An unknown voice took my call and told me that our guest had just suffered a heart attack and could not attend the lunch. Surmising that the illness was diplomatic and that our guest had been instructed by higher-ups not to attend, I called again the next day and our delinquent guest himself answered the phone. After expressing my regrets about his failure to show, I congratulated him on his speedy recovery and wished him continued good health.

Vranyo can also be used at high levels of government. In August 1991, during the attempted Moscow coup, Westerners wondered why so many apparently healthy Russian leaders, including Gorbachev, were said to be ill and unavailable, only to surface in a few days looking quite healthy.

In December 1994 the Russian military was accused of assisting rebels who were attempting to topple the government of Chechnya, the Muslim republic in the Caucasus that had declared independence from the Russian Federation. Moscow denied the accusation, and when Russian soldiers in Chechnya were captured by Chechen forces, Moscow officials, including Defense Minister Grachev, claimed that the captured soldiers were mercenaries. But when the soldiers admitted on Chechen television that they were members of a Russian military unit sent secretly to Chechnya by the KGB, the Russian Defense Ministry was forced to concede that they were indeed Russian military personnel.

Vranyo can even show up at summit meetings. During their May 1995 Moscow Summit, President Yeltsin assured President Bill Clinton, as reported in *The New York Times*, that "there are no military actions going on in Chechnya," adding that "the

130

Interior Ministry is now simply confiscating weapons still in the hands of small rebel bands" (11 May 1995). Shortly after Boris Yeltsin spoke, the media reported that Russian helicopters were attacking Chechen villages, firing rockets into farmhouses.

When the Russian nuclear submarine *Kursk*, with a crew of 118, sank in August 2000, the Russian navy issued a series of misstatements that downplayed the seriousness of the accident, were patently false, and raised false hopes among the families of the victims.[†]

The navy initially reported the accident on Monday, August 14, saying it had taken place on Sunday; in fact, it had occurred on Saturday. The navy said the *Kursk* was crippled by "technical faults," and the crew had allowed it to glide to the seabed; actually, it was destroyed by explosions on board; it flooded quickly and sank, and most of the crew died within minutes. A navy spokesman said rescuers were in radio contact with the crew; in fact, there was no radio contact from the moment of the accident. The navy also said that the crew had immediately signaled that it had shut down the nuclear reactor, but officials later said that the reactors had been closed down automatically; in fact, the navy had no information from on board. Officials also denied that the submarine was flooded, adding that there was no damage to the hull. The next day, Tuesday, August 15, the navy announced that the crew had signaled that there had been no deaths on board and officially denied that there had been some deaths. One day later, Wednesday, August 16, a high-ranking navy officer said the crew was continuing to send signals by tapping on the hull; officials later announced that the last sound from the vessel had come on Monday. Finally, on Saturday, August 19, the navy acknowledged that damage to the sub had been massive, most of the crew had died within minutes, and the others were certainly dead. Admirals and politicians, however, began to circulate a story that an American or

[†] I have drawn here from a Reuter's dispatch from Moscow, 21 August 2000, reported in *Johnson's Russia List*, #4467.

British submarine had collided with the *Kursk*. It was not until almost two years later that a Russian commission investigating the disaster acknowledged that the *Kursk* had not collided with another sub or stray mine but had been sunk by an explosion of one of its own torpedoes.

Related to vranyo is *pokazukha*, the tradition of staging an event "for show," especially for high officials and visiting foreign dignitaries. The classic example is the "Potemkin village," named after one of Empress Catherine the Great's favorites. According to legend, false village facades were constructed along the travel route of the empress to show Catherine how well her people were living. Pokazukha was continued in the Soviet era when life was portrayed as the government wanted it to be seen, not as it actually was. The Soviets, for example, staged the opening of the Baikal-Amur Railway in 1984, the target year for its completion, although the huge project was far from being finished at the time.

If Russians are compelled by tradition to show only the best, Americans seem obliged to show the worst. As one Russian reported after visiting the United States, everywhere he went his American hosts showed him what was wrong, but they also told him what was being done to correct matters. By showing what is wrong, Americans are reflecting their optimism about being able to change things for the better. Russians, by showing the best, are revealing their embarrassment about shortcomings in their society, their inability to deal with them openly, and their pessimism for the future. "America is about success," writes Richard Lourie, "Russia about survival" (1991, 2).

At times Russians may say something that an American finds patently wrong or unacceptable. Some Americans, preferring to avoid a confrontation, will choose to let the matter pass. But remaining silent in such a situation may create an impression of acquiescence that would be misleading. Depending on the importance of the issue under discussion, it may be preferable to point out the error, even if it should lead to controversy. Russians will respect you if you are candid and straightforward.

132

If your facts are true, Russians will not be offended by being corrected. They will also not hesitate to correct an American, and their criticism should be accepted in the same spirit. This is a trait Russians and Americans share.

Nyekulturno

Instruction shapes your mind; upbringing, your manners.
—Russian proverb

Coats and other outerwear must be checked on entering office buildings, theaters, concert halls, restaurants, museums, and other public buildings in Russia. In the lobbies of those buildings visitors will find a *garderob* (cloakroom) staffed by one or more of those ubiquitous Russian grandmothers. The checking procedure is efficient and dependable, and tipping is not customary. The mandatory checking of outer garments makes good sense because people must bundle up in cold weather. But be sure that your coat has a loop sewn into it for hanging or you will be berated by the garderob personnel.

Everyday Russian life is full of other dos and don'ts, reflecting the state's efforts to impose patterns of behavior on a newly urbanized citizenry only recently removed from their tradition-bound villages. There is a right way and a wrong way to do almost everything, and Russians will not hesitate to tell you when you are doing something wrong. The wrong way is termed *nyekulturno* (uncultured, bad manners, or vulgar), and a foreign visitor's behavior will be judged by the same standards.

Wearing coats in public buildings is nyekulturno, although Russians see nothing wrong in strolling through hotel corridors clad only in pajamas or bathrobes, as if the hotel were a large communal apartment. Also nyekulturno are standing with hands in pants pockets, sprawling in chairs, placing feet on tables, crossing legs while seated so as to show the sole of a shoe, sitting with legs spread wide, crossing arms behind the head, draping an arm over the back of a chair, or merely lounging. People are expected to behave in public with a degree of decorum. These are not exclusively Russian attitudes; disdain for such demeanor may be found in other European countries as well.

Many other liberties are also nyekulturno. Students do not eat, drink, or chew gum during class. Eating lunch on park lawns in the city is unacceptable. In the evening, theater patrons are expected to dress appropriately for opera, theater, and the symphony.

When you are going into a theater aisle to reach your seat, turn to face the seated people you will be passing, rather than showing them your backside. Loud talk in public and being "pushy" are taboo; the quiet "sell" and modesty will get you further. Telling Russians that you have to go to the rest room is also nyekulturno. Simply excuse yourself; they'll know where you are going.

Russian performers, public speakers, and others on stage will join their audiences in applause, a move that puzzles some visitors. They are, however, not applauding their own performance but are expressing approval and appreciation of the spectators and their response to the performance.

And I have had to explain to high-ranking visiting officials that whistling in a concert hall after a performance is not showing approval; rather, it is a sign of disapproval in Russia (and elsewhere in Europe).

Time and Patience

> Punctuality has been exceedingly difficult to instill into a population unused to regular hours.
> —Margaret Mead, *Soviet Attitudes toward Authority*

Time is money to some nationalities, and punctuality, a virtue. Meetings are expected to start on time, and work under pressure of the clock is a challenge routinely accepted. To Russians, however, with their agricultural heritage, time is like the seasons—a time to reap, a time to sow, and a time for doing little in between.

Seychas budyit (it will be done right away) is an expression heard often in Russia, from waiters in restaurants, clerks in stores, and officials in offices. Be assured, however, that whatever has been promised will not be done right away but will more likely take some time.

Communism reinforced the native Russian disrespect for time, because workers could not be fired, and there was no incentive to do things on time. Moreover, in a country where time is not a vital commodity, people become more sanguine about accepting delays. When something very important must be done, it will be done, and time and cost will not be obstacles. But time for Russians is not yet an economic commodity to be measured in rubles or dollars.

Being on time is consequently alien. Russians are notoriously late, and they think nothing of arriving long after the appointed hour, which is not considered as being late. (Concerts and theater performances, however, do start on time, and latecomers will not be seated until the first intermission.)

When Russians do arrive, there are a number of rituals that must be played out before the business part of a meeting can start. First, the small talk, a necessary part of all personal encounters; then, the customary tea or other drink, followed perhaps by conversation about family and personal problems; and finally, the business of the day. All this takes time, and the meeting usually does not start before ten o'clock in the morning.

The business part of the talk will also be lengthy because important issues are approached in a roundabout rather than direct manner. Impatient foreign businesspeople often wonder when the key issues of the meeting will be discussed. And after the meeting has concluded and the visitor believes an agreement to proceed has been reached, nothing may happen for weeks, or months, or ever.

For Russians, time is not measured in minutes or hours but more likely in days, weeks, and months. The venerated virtue is not punctuality but patience. As a student from India who had spent four years in Moscow advised me, "Be patient, hope for the best, but prepare for the worst. Everything here takes time and sometimes never gets done."

Americans and some Northern Europeans are oriented toward doing; Russians are accustomed to contemplating. As a Russian psychiatrist explained to me, "Russians can look at an object all day and reflect on it but take no action." When faced with an issue to be resolved, they will first think through the historical, philosophical, and ideological considerations as well as the consequences of whatever is to be decided. "Doers" will first consider the practical points, the obstacles to overcome, the details, and how to get from here to there.

A Russian conference interpreter, recalling her experience with Russians and Americans in the evenings after their formal meetings had adjourned, told me, "The Russians would sit all night drinking tea, discussing and reflecting, while the Americans would be thinking about what they had to do the next day and preparing to do it."

Such divergent views of time can create difficulties in cooperative efforts and joint ventures. Americans will want to negotiate an agreement expeditiously, schedule an early start on the venture, begin on time, meet production deadlines, complete the work as promptly as possible, and show early results or profit. Russians will need more time to get organized, and there will be frequent delays and postponements. They will be less concerned with immediate results, and profit is a concept that they are only beginning to understand. The job may be completed but only after considerable prodding from the American side.

What to do? Not much, except to persist patiently, and speak softly but carry a big prod. Once prodded, and made to understand that a deadline must be met, Russians can show prodigious bursts of energy and will work around the clock to complete the job.

The Russian Language

The Russian language surpasses all European languages, since it has the magnificence of Spanish, the liveliness of French, the

strength of German, the delicacy of Italian, as well as the rich-
ness and conciseness of Greek and Latin.

—M. V. Lomonosov

Foreigners most successful in understanding the Russians, as
readers will have noted by now, are those who speak some
Russian. Speakers of Russian, be they businesspeople, journalists, scholars, scientists, or professional or citizen diplomats, all
have a significant advantage. Communication may be possible
through smiles, hand signals, body language, and interpreters,
but the ability to carry on a conversation in Russian raises the
relationship to a more meaningful level.

Those who are put off by the challenge of studying Russian
should know that it is far easier to learn than many other languages such as Chinese, Arabic, or Finnish. Russians, moreover,
are not offended by foreigners with an inadequate command of
Russian. Many of their own citizens also speak Russian poorly.

The study of Russian in the United States has declined dras-
tically since the end of the Cold War. In 1993, some 14,700
students were enrolled in precollege study of Russian, but by
2000 there were only 6,700. In 1990 there were 44,384 college
students of Russian, but by 1998 only 24,000. As Russians have
often pointed out, there were more teachers of English in the
Soviet Union (about 100,000) than students of Russian in the
U.S.

How to explain this? There is some speculation that the
decline in Russian language study is an element in the "peace
dividend." As possibilities for U.S.-Russian conflict decline, so
does interest in Russian language study in the United States. That
defies logic, of course, since reform in Russia and the improve-
ment in U.S.-Russian relations open up many opportunities for
Americans to interact with Russians.

Russian is a Slavic language, together with Ukrainian, Belaru-
sian, Polish, Czech, Slovak, Bulgarian, and several other related
tongues. They are all Indo-European languages, a group that
includes, among others, the Germanic, Romance, and English
languages, all of which have common roots.

Russian and English with common roots? While this at first may seem difficult to imagine, Russian and English do have many cognates—related words with a common root. That most basic word *milk*, for example, is a cognate of the German *milch*, Polish *mleko*, and Russian *moloko*. Compare also *apple* with the German *apfel*, Polish *jablko* (pronounced "yablkoh") and Russian *yabloko*. Notice also that the words become longer, adding a syllable or two as they travel east from English and German to Polish and Russian. Perhaps this is why English has so many four-letter words.

It takes about 10 to 15 percent longer to say something in Russian than in English, and experienced translators say that they will often need three or more Russian words for one English word. Add to this the Russian tendency to be long-winded—a characteristic of agricultural societies—and you have another reason for Russian verbosity.

Further difficulty with Russian results from the shifting accentuation of words. There is no general rule on where the stress falls in a word or sentence, as there is in most European languages, but a Russian word placed at the beginning of a sentence will have more importance than when placed at the end.

The Cyrillic alphabet, named after St. Cyril, the apostle to the Slavs who devised the Glagolithic alphabet on which Cyrillic is based, may also worry some students. Russian, however, is pronounced as it is written. If you can read Cyrillic, you can pronounce it. This gives Russian an advantage over English, where words are seldom pronounced as they are written.

Foreigners who do not speak Russian should at least learn the Cyrillic alphabet before traveling to Russia. Familiarity with its thirty-two letters will enable travelers to read signs, menus, and the names of Metro stations and will considerably facilitate a pleasant stay. It will also give them a start in building a Russian vocabulary. A basic vocabulary can be easily acquired by learning a few root words and the Russian equivalents of English prefixes, suffixes, and prepositions. Moreover, many of those long and imposing Russian words are structured exactly as their Western equivalents are.

Russian has numerous words acquired from Western languages. Many mechanical, medical, and technical terms are from German; artistic and cultural words from French; and business and modern scientific terms from English. More recently, many English words, previously unknown in Russia, have also come into common usage—*kserokopiya* (xerox copy), *faks* (fax), *mikser* (mixer), *forvardy* (forward), *optsiony* (options), *dzhinsy* (jeans), *keeleri* (contract killers), and *biznesmeni* (businessmen)—although they are given a Russian pronunciation and often a Slavic ending.

Words are inflected, as in Latin and German, to denote such distinctions as case, gender, number, tense, person, and mood. And Russian verbs have two aspects—the imperfective for repeated actions, and the perfective for completed actions. Hingley wonders, facetiously, whether it is not this strict separation of these two aspects of the verb that makes it so difficult for Russians to complete actions (1977, 206). The grammar seems complex, and it is, but there are a few rules that explain it all. Although Russian can be learned cold, it helps to know another inflected European language.

Russian is also replete with negatives, and even positive ideas are often expressed negatively. An object will be "not big" rather than "small." A Russian will describe his or her feelings as "not bad" rather than "good." And a double negative in Russian does not make an affirmative as in English; it merely emphasizes the negative. The more negatives in a sentence, the more negative the meaning.

One final caveat: while Russian has its share of earthy and vulgar expressions, they are not used in polite society.

Misunderstandings

There are two ways you can tell when a man is lying. One is when he says he can drink champagne all night and not get drunk. The other is when he says he understands Russians.
—Charles E. Bohlen, former U.S. ambassador to Moscow

Russian is a very rich language. Whereas in English one word may suffice to convey an idea, Russian will have several words to choose from, each with a slightly different shade of meaning. This presents problems for interpreters and translators, as well as possibilities for misunderstandings.

Many words and expressions in one language simply do not exist in the other. Aleksei Mikhalev, a Russian translator of American literature, says that differences in language and literature—two significant products of a nation's thought and psychology—demonstrate that English speakers and Russians are not very much alike. He cites the impossibility of finding precise Russian equivalents for the simple English word *privacy*, a concept that does not exist in Russian nor in many other languages, for that matter. Other untranslatables from English to Russian listed by Mikhalev include *take care, have fun, make love, efficiency,* and *challenge* (in Lourie and Mikhalev 1989, 38).

Even translatable words are sometimes mistranslated, especially when idiomatic language is involved. Kornei Chukovsky, one of the best translators from English into Russian, has cited several such bloopers. In one, an experienced Russian translator, translating a work by American poet Langston Hughes, wrote about the passionate love of a black man for a black woman who had rejected him. Actually, Hughes had written about a "Black Maria" (police van) that he hoped was not coming to get him.

Another example cited by Chukovsky, from John Galsworthy's *The Forsyte Saga*, had a young man, Michael Mont, rowing a boat with his girlfriend across a river when he suddenly "caught a crab" (a rowing term indicating a faulty stroke). The Russian translator had Mont fishing for crabs in the middle of an ardent conversation with his sweetheart (1984, 11–12).

Seemingly simple expressions can have one meaning in English and another in Russian, as I learned when helping to arrange the first loan between a Russian and American museum. In 1973, the National Gallery of Art in Washington, D.C., sought to borrow a Rembrandt from Moscow's Pushkin Museum. In the spirit of detente, the Soviet government agreed to lend the work, but it first sought assurance that the U.S. government would guarantee the security of the valuable Rembrandt while it was in the United States.

In response to an official request for a guarantee, I informed the Soviet cultural attaché that the State Department would take "all possible measures" to safeguard the Rembrandt. That was boilerplate language used to indicate that the department would do all it possibly could—in this case merely requesting the museum and local authorities to take appropriate measures to protect the Rembrandt. The Soviet diplomat then asked, in Russian, whether that meant *vsyo vozmozhnoye* (everything possible), an expression that is stronger in Russian than in English, with the emphasis on "everything." I repeated, in English, that the State Department would take all possible measures. My Russian colleague accepted that as vsyo vozmozhnoye, which satisfied Moscow's needs. Had the Rembrandt been damaged or stolen, it might have been the end of his career, and mine.

To prevent misunderstandings, anyone planning to give an oral presentation to Russians should also present a paper containing the principal points covered in the talk. A written statement will help to avoid the hazards of interpreting as well as the tendency of Russians to think in general rather than specific terms. Presenting a paper also ensures that Russians will know exactly what the visitor intended to say, regardless of what was actually said and how it was translated into Russian.

Communication Differences

Russia has an oral rather than a written tradition—understandable in a country where most of the people were illiterate less than a century ago—and talk comes naturally to its people. Every Russian seems to be a born orator. Conversations begin easily between complete strangers and also between men and women. The complexities of the language notwithstanding, it can be a pleasure to listen to Russian speech. Delivery is unhurried, often eloquent, and without pretense. But Russians may also talk around a difficult issue without addressing it directly. Listeners should pay close attention to what is left unsaid in addition to what is said. As Lyudmila Putin, wife of the president, once told a German friend, "You must always listen between the words and read between the lines" (2001).

Don't expect short responses to simple questions. The question-and-answer approach simply will not do. Rather than respond with a brief yes or no, Russians are more likely to give a lengthy explanation that will leave the listener wondering whether the answer is indeed yes or no. David Remnick recalls how this worked, in an interview with Gorbachev. "I asked a question, and he finished his answer forty minutes later..." (1992, 120).

Nyet is a simple Russian word that is often misunderstood—an almost automatic response by Russians when asked if something can be done. Clerks, doormen, officials, and others seem to prefer the easy response, "Nyet."

There can be several reasons for the automatic nyet. One common explanation is "We don't do it that way here." Or the item requested in a store or restaurant may indeed not be available. Or the clerk may not care whether it is available or may not be at all interested in helping the customer. In any event Russians do not routinely accept a nyet, and neither should you. Continue talking, keep your cool, don't raise your voice, and keep repeating your request. As noted before, a good interpersonal relationship can often overcome the obstacle, whatever it may be, and beat the system.

A nyet, however, when expressed in a manner indicating that the real response is "perhaps," may indicate that a little incentive is needed. In such cases, a few dollars, discreetly brought into view, may produce the desired effect.

Body language is also important. Russians use hands and facial expressions to express ideas and emotions, in contrast to Anglo-Saxons, who consider such demeanor distracting if not unmannerly. Through body language, a person's intent can be determined without even understanding the words. Facial expressions are also clues to behavior. Russians tend to start out with grim faces, but when they do smile, it reflects relaxation and progress in developing a good relationship. Winks and nods are also good signs. If a stony look continues, however, it means you are not getting through and are in trouble.

Physical contact by Russians—touching another person—is a sign that things are going well and that a degree of rapport has been reached. The degree of physical contact will indicate how well things are going. If a Russian places a hand on your arm, for example, or embraces you, you can relax a bit; these are good signs.

Closeness and physical contact with other persons, as noted above, are much more common in Russia than in the West, a heritage of the village past when people lived in close proximity in small huts. Russians also stand very close when conversing, often less than twelve inches apart, which is closer than many Westerners will find comfortable. They gesticulate more and do not hesitate to make physical contact and invade the other person's space.

A visiting teacher of Russian recalls how, during study at Moscow State University, a Russian instructor playfully rapped the knuckles of some Americans in his class as a sign of displeasure over their inadequate preparation for the day's lesson:

> The American men, in an uproar at both the teacher's invasion of their space and his use of body contact to enforce his wishes, went immediately after class to the director to complain about the instructor's behavior.... As a result, the instructor was reprimanded and told to maintain "a proper distance" from his students and to refrain from all physical contact with Americans, "who do not understand these things." (Monahan 1983, 15)

There are times, however, when Russian knuckles should be rapped. "The Russian is never more agreeable than after his knuckles have been sharply rapped," writes George F. Kennan.

"He takes well to rough play and rarely holds grudges over it" (1967, 564).

Straight talk is appreciated, even when it leads to disagreement. When disagreement does occur, Russians appreciate honesty rather than attempts to paper over differences. It is far better to level with them and be certain that they fully understand your position. They respect adversaries who are straightforward and sincere in expressing views that diverge from their own.

Secretary of State Colin Powell, en route to a meeting with Russian foreign minister Igor S. Ivanov, recalled his long record of interaction with Russian leaders over the years as national security adviser and chairman of the Joint Chiefs of Staff in the first Bush administration. "If one speaks openly and candidly," he said in an article in *The New York Times*, "you can make progress as long as you don't shy away from the tough issues and as long as you don't forget that there are many areas of interest that we have in common" (25 February 2001).

But confrontations over differences of views can often be avoided by letting Russians talk themselves out. After they have expressed their righteousness and indignation and have unburdened themselves, their opposition may moderate, and the differences may turn out to be less than originally believed. In fact, after talking themselves out, Russians and Westerners may even find that they have a unanimity of views.

The Telephone

> Telephones in Russia are enough to make the most patient man curse.
> —Irving R. Levine, *Main Street, U.S.S.R.*

Irving R. Levine was NBC correspondent in Moscow in the 1950s, but his description of the Russian telephone system may still be valid in many parts of the country. Service in Moscow, St. Petersburg, and a few other cities is good and comparable with the West, but in smaller cities and rural areas, the service

is inadequate, the technology is ancient, and the cursing continues.

The Russian telephone system underwent significant changes
in the 1990s as it made progress toward building the telecommunications infrastructure necessary for a market economy.
More than one thousand companies are now licensed to offer
communications services, access to digital lines has improved
in urban centers, Internet and e-mail services are available, and
cybercafés have sprung up in major cities. However, the large
demand for telephone service remains unsatisfied, and in many
cities there is a long wait to have a home phone installed.

Despite advances in technology, Russians, belonging to a culture that values personal relations, still prefer to communicate
face-to-face; doing business from a distance can therefore be
difficult. Letters are answered late, if at all. Communications
through fax and e-mail may get a better response, but that is
by no means assured. So, what do you need to know about using the telephone, the preferred medium for communication in
the West?

First, know your number. For many years there was no Moscow
telephone directory. One was eventually published in 1990, but
only 250,000 copies were printed, a mere drop in the bucket for a
city of more than ten million. Now, directories are published for
business and government phones, and there are Yellow Pages in
English. Directories are also available on the Internet, but before
departing for Moscow it is advisable to obtain from earlier travelers the numbers of people you will be trying to reach. And when
you are in Moscow, carry a "little black book" wherever you go,
and write down the numbers of people you may want to contact
later. Public phones that work with a telephone card are also
available. Cards may be purchased at Metro stations and other
sites and can be used to call anywhere in Russia or the world.

Cell phones are becoming increasingly popular in Moscow
and other large cities, but Russians can be just as rude, if not
ruder, than Americans when using them. Luncheon discussions,
where considerable business is conducted, may be interrupted

by the ringing of a cell phone, which is then followed by the person you're supposed to be having lunch with talking to someone else.

It may also come as a surprise to learn that many Russian officials do not mind being called at home. In fact, many of them have their office and home phone numbers on their *vizitnaya* calling card.

One Soviet writer's surprised reaction to how Americans use the telephone tells us as much about Russia as it does about the United States. After visiting the U.S. he wrote,

> One rarely hears of business meetings in the United States. All matters are settled straightaway on the spot, by telephone. Whichever establishment you call you may be sure that the man you want will be available. If, for some important reason, he's not there, a secretary will answer and will always tell you affably and politely who can help you instead, or will tell you exactly when the person you need will be back and when you should call him. The most complex questions are settled by telephone. (Laurinciukas 1977, 175)

Russians and Americans

> You Russians and we Americans! Our countries so distant, so unlike at first glance—such a difference in social and political conditions, and our respective methods of moral and practical development the last hundred years—and yet in certain features, and vastest ones, so resembling each other.
> —Walt Whitman, *Letter to a Russian*

Despite Russia's ambivalence toward the West, and notwithstanding the political and cultural differences and the often diametrically opposed values of the two societies, most Russians like Americans.

"The foreign country in which the majority of Russians...are most interested is America," wrote Sir William Hayter, a former British ambassador to Moscow. "It is the goal they are constantly being urged, or urging themselves, to 'catch up and overtake.' They share many tastes with it—love of gadgets, technology, massive scale.... America is their favorite foreign country" (1966, 133).

During my own service in Moscow with the American Embassy at the height of the Vietnam War, I never once met a Russian who held anything against me as an American. How could that be, given our differences then and the steady stream of anti-American propaganda that Russians were fed in their media over so many decades?

To begin with, the effect of anti-American propaganda should be discounted. Until glasnost, few Russians believed what their media told them. If news was official, it was doubted; if a rumor, it was believed. Russians have had good reason to question official pronouncements.

In a country whose thousand-year history records one war after another—and with immense suffering—Russians know that they have never had a war with the United States. They also know that Russians and Americans were allies against their most recent enemy, Germany, in two world wars. Moreover, there are no territorial disputes between the two countries, a common cause of conflict.

Russia and the United States have no trade rivalries, nor do they compete in world markets. Many Russians also recall the aid they received from the U.S.—during the famine of the 1920s, the industrialization of the 1920s and 1930s, and the lend-lease of the 1940s during the darkest days of their life-and-death struggle with Nazi Germany. Indeed, some Soviet military vehicles were commonly known in Russian as "Willys" and "Studebakers" because the first jeeps and trucks to arrive from the U.S. during the war bore the names of those companies.

Fascination with machinery is shared by Russians and Americans. The best way to start a conversation with Russians, as I learned in Moscow, was to open the hood of my American station wagon on a downtown street and start tinkering with the engine. Immediately, I would be surrounded by a crowd asking how many "horses" the engine had, how fast the car could go, how much gas it used (in liters per hundred kilometers), and how much it cost.

But to go beyond casual conversation and really get to know Russians, you must sit down with them and eat and drink together. The best conversations with Russians occur, as earlier noted, at the kitchen table. The highlight of a visit to the United States by a delegation of senior Russian officials occurred when they sat around a kitchen table with American farmers in the Midwest and discussed farming far into the night.

I had a similar experience once when I dropped in unannounced at the library of the Siberian Academy of Sciences in Novosibirsk. Identifying myself as the cultural counselor of the American Embassy, I asked to see the library director. Surprised by the unexpected visit of an American diplomat, he graciously ushered me into his office. The legendary Russian hospitality soon showed itself when he sent an assistant out to get something for us to eat. She returned shortly with a long spicy sausage, a loaf of good black bread, a bottle of vodka, and an old kitchen knife; our conversation warmed with our stomachs as we sat at his desk eating and drinking—without plates, forks, or napkins—and discussing libraries and book exchanges between our two countries. (His main complaint was that most of the books that the country received from abroad stayed in Moscow and did not reach Siberia.)

America's power and size also attract Russians—the "big is beautiful" syndrome. Russians see themselves and Americans as citizens of two great powers destined to play leading roles on the world stage. As a Russian professor explained to me, "We have more in common with Americans than with West Europeans. Both our countries have no aristocracies, both are big and without the complexes of small nations."

Joint endeavors between Russians and Americans are therefore seen as natural. Indeed, Russians get a psychological lift from working with Americans, regarding such cooperation as recognition of their coequal status. But they also expect Americans to

148

accept them as equals, to return their admiration, and they are disappointed and puzzled when we do not.

One standard Russian complaint against Americans, writes Eliza Klose, is that they lack *dusha*, or soul:

> Many [in the former Soviet Union] believe that for all their welcoming smiles and quick friendliness, Americans are too pre-occupied with earning a living to make the kind of long-term commitments to others that people in the former Soviet Union equate with friendship and cultural depth. (1994, 2)

Americans may indeed lack soul; nevertheless, Russians are very curious about the United States, and there is no country they wish to visit more. Many exciting innovations in their lives have come from America—jazz, jeans, Coke and Pepsi, and Big Macs, to name a few. Russians who were able to visit the States during the Soviet years were astounded by the abundance they found there and the high standard of living. On seeing their first American supermarket, many believed it to be a "Potemkin village," a setup created to impress foreigners. Others, confused by the choices offered to consumers, questioned the need for so many different brands of the same product.

Russians recognize that Americans are far richer than they are, but they resent being talked down to. While Russians themselves are outspokenly critical of their own society, they can be hypersensitive to criticism by a foreigner. As one Russian teacher told me, "We think of America as the rich cousin, who has material wealth, meeting Russia, the poor cousin, who has spiritual wealth. We are envious of your material wealth, but don't flaunt it. We know you have it."

Much of what Russians see in the United States puzzles them—the free choices, the seeming lack of order, the concern for individual rights, the decay of its great cities, and the decentralization of the economy. Indeed, some Russians, after touring the U.S., have been certain that there must be some secret center that controls and runs the economy. How else could it perform so well?

To Americans, Russians are also puzzling. Why is it so difficult and time-consuming to reach agreement with them? Why do they always seem to be delaying decisions instead of being reasonable? Why are they so mistrustful of others, and can they be trusted to honor agreements? Despite some similarities, Russians and Americans are indeed different, Walt Whitman's words notwithstanding. Familiarization with the differences is the first step to bridging them.

Familiarity, however, can also breed contempt. Criticism of the West, and the United States in particular, is now heard across the Russian political spectrum but mainly among the political elite, some of whom believe that the U.S. deliberately set out to destroy the Soviet Union, first through Gorbachev and then through Yeltsin. Others blame the U.S. for the dislocations caused by the drastic drop in their standard of living, precipitous decline of social services, rapid deterioration of public health, and sharp increases in crime, violence, and corruption.

Many Russians resent the large influx of Americans and other Westerners who have descended on Moscow and give it the appearance of a boomtown. Foreigners no longer live in isolated enclaves, nor do they shop in exclusive, hard-currency-only supermarkets containing a wide range of Western products. All goods in Russia must now be sold for rubles, and Western products are available to all in stores across Moscow and other major cities, although at prices beyond the reach of most Russians. The range and quality of such products have made many Russians resentful of foreigners, as have the small class of Russian businesspeople and mafia who flaunt their own affluence and high lifestyles.

In a similar vein, Vladimir Putin's forging of closer relations with the United States and his cooperation with NATO have aroused opposition from many Russians across the political spectrum as well as from the Russian military.

America bashing has become politically popular.

6

Negotiating with Russians

If there are found among the Russians, better diplomatists than among other nations...it is because our journals inform them of every thing which is done or projected among ourselves, and because instead of prudently disguising our weaknesses, we display them, with passion, every morning; whilst, on the contrary, the Byzantine policy of the Russians, working in the dark, carefully conceals from us everything that is thought, done, or feared among them. We march exposed on all sides, they advance under cover. The ignorance in which they leave us blinds our view; our sincerity enlightens theirs; we suffer from all the evils of idle talking, they have all the advantages of secrecy; and herein lies all their skill and ability....

—Marquis de Custine, *Empire of the Czar*

The Art of Negotiation

Don't hurry to reply, but hurry to listen.

—Russian proverb

Negotiation is an art well known to diplomats, lawyers, and business executives. Two parties meet, each with its own objectives, and attempt to reach a mutually acceptable agreement that will satisfy their basic needs. The goal for each side is to gain as much as possible while giving up only what is necessary to reach agreement. At this age-old game the Russians are experts, in part because they are not in a hurry.

151

Where the two sides have similar goals, as is often the case when negotiations are entered into willingly, the process can be relatively easy. Both sides seek to reach agreement and have hopes of doing so; otherwise, they would not have agreed to meet. But when Russians and Americans negotiate, there are often considerations that may make it difficult to agree.

For the United States and Russia, the negotiation of minor issues may be amplified out of proportion because of their rivalry, thereby making minor issues appear more important than they really are. Agreement in principle on broad objectives may be easy to reach, but how the agreement will be carried out—the details of implementation—are usually more difficult. Long-standing policy may have to be modified by one side or the other. The terms of the agreement must satisfy the legal, political, and ideological requirements of both sides—yes, Americans may also have ideological considerations. And the subject under negotiation may be related to other issues for which one side or the other may not wish to establish a precedent.

Most Americans who negotiate with Russians represent only themselves or their organizations, while the Russians in negotiations may also represent their government or need government approval before signing. Russian negotiators, moreover, are likely to be under strict instructions and without the flexibility of their American opposites to make on-the-spot decisions. Where the negotiators represent private entities, they will have more flexibility.

The greatest challenge, however, results from the different Russian and American approaches to negotiations. Americans generally regard compromise as desirable and inevitable, a logical way of conducting business—meet them halfway and make a deal. Americans, consequently, regard any inability to reach agreement easily and quickly as failure. Russians regard compromise as a sign of weakness, a retreat from a correct and morally justified position. Russians, therefore, are great "sitters," prepared to wait out their opposite numbers in the expectation that time and Russian patience will produce more concessions from the impatient Americans. Soviet Foreign Minister Vyacheslav Molotov was dubbed "Stonebottom" because of his ability to outsit the other side.

Chess is a Russian national pastime, and Russians negotiate in the same way as they play chess, planning several moves ahead. Americans should think through the consequences of each move before making it, since it may establish a precedent that the Russians will cite later on, or it may lead to a tack in the negotiations different from the one expected.

Russian negotiating teams are usually composed of veterans who negotiate year round with representatives of other countries. Americans, products of a mobile society, are more likely to be new to their positions and less experienced in the art of negotiation, particularly with Russians.

A concept or word from one side of the table may not be understood by the other because it simply does not exist in the other side's politics, laws, culture, or even language. Add to this the limitations to what Americans and Russians know and understand about each other, and the task of negotiating becomes even more challenging.

Equality, reciprocity, and mutual advantage are watchwords that need to be kept in mind. Russians and Americans negotiate as equals, and Russians are very sensitive to any intimations that they are not being treated with sufficient respect and dignity. Agreements reached should provide for reciprocity—what is done in one country should be matched by similar action in the other, and under conditions as equal as possible. And most important, the benefits to each side should be comparable.

The negotiations can be lengthy, tedious, and demanding. Negotiation, however, is the only way to do business with Russians—a handshake alone will not do—and Americans should understand the basic rules of the game before entering the playing field.

Procedures and Tactics

Where there is sense, there is order.
—Russian proverb

The first step in any negotiation is to know what you want. That may sound overly simple but often it is not. Many negotiators go into meetings without knowing precisely what their objectives are. Americans had better think through their objectives and define them clearly, because the Russians will certainly know their own.

The next step is to draft the text of an agreement that includes all your objectives. This is your maximum position—what you ideally would like to see in the final document. The Russians will also have their draft, with their objectives, and it will represent their maximum position. Each side should understand that this is merely the opening bid—as in an Eastern bazaar—and neither should expect the other to accept the initial draft it has placed on the table. To save time, drafts may be exchanged in advance of the actual negotiations so that each side may study the other's objectives and draft language and be better prepared to negotiate.

Russian negotiating strategy reflects differences in thought patterns between East and West. Western negotiators prefer a pragmatic and detailed approach, taking up one issue at a time and progressing systematically toward a final agreement. Russians prefer a more general and conceptual approach, without specificity.

In political negotiations, for example, Russians will often seek agreement "in principle," which will be in harmony with an ideological framework or universal outlook. Such an agreement, which provides greater flexibility when the time for implementation arrives, will include high-sounding ideals couched in lofty language, but few details. You should start with simple proposals and develop the complexities later, but not so late that they may be considered by the Russians insufficiently important to be taken seriously. If numbers are important, they should be specified and their importance emphasized. Russians are often inexact when it comes to numbers, unless the subject is rubles/dollars, in which case Russians will be sticklers for detail, insisting on a more detailed contract than is usual in international business.

The protocol of who sits where at the negotiating table should be observed, as Russians are very status conscious. The Russian head of delegation may sit at the center of the table, flanked on both sides by an interpreter and aides in descending order of rank. Or the chairperson may sit at the head of the table. Whatever the arrangement, you should match it, with your chairperson seated across from his or her Russian counterpart. The two chairpersons should be of comparable rank, and a high-ranking visitor will be taken more seriously.

In their opening statement, Russians will provide a philosophical or ideological basis for their negotiating position. The opening statement may also provide clues to specific positions they will take later on and reveal previously unstated objectives or difficulties that were not anticipated.

In the give-and-take of negotiations, Russians will attempt to size up their opposite number. Who is this person? Is he or she serious, strong, trustworthy? In making this assessment, Russians, like boxers, will bob and weave, feint and probe for weaknesses, and press forward vigorously when they sense a willingness from the other side to accommodate their views. When a probe meets with resistance, they will pull back and regroup.

Russian delivery style can be dramatic and emotional, intended to demonstrate true commitment to the position being espoused. Tough talk may also be used to beat down adversaries. Russians can raise their voices, express indignation, and imply threats. This behavior should be seen for what it actually is—theatrics—although it also reflects a Russian propensity for power plays.

You can respond in two ways; you can allow the Russians to speak their piece, hear them out, enjoy the performance, and respond in a firm but calm manner; alternatively, you may elect to talk tough as well, which Russians will understand and respect as an indication of resolve and determination. Because he did not understand this, President John F. Kennedy gave Premier Nikita Khrushchev the impression, when they met in Vienna in 1961, that he was weak and could be intimidated by the emplacement of Soviet missiles in Cuba.

In most negotiations Russians maintain strict discipline and speak with one voice, that of their delegation chairperson. An exception to this rule may be found in commercial or other negotiations where several government ministries or agencies are represented on the Russian side, along with end users. Americans, by contrast, tend to speak with many voices, reflecting the pluralism of U.S. society as well as disparate views within the delegation. This confuses Russians because they do not know which American is speaking with authority, though they will be quick to exploit any perceived differences.

The most difficult part of a negotiation, Americans often report, is reaching agreement among the various viewpoints and interests of their own side. Any such differences should be resolved in advance, and Americans should speak with one voice at the negotiating table, remembering their national motto, E pluribus unum.

The choice of the language used may become an issue. Russians will usually request that official negotiations, or at least plenary sessions (with full delegations), be conducted in both languages, even when the Russian negotiators speak English well. Russians regard their language as a world language on a par with English. The French and many others do the same. In small working groups, however, negotiations may be held in English.

One or more members of the U.S. delegation should be designated as note taker. Not everything that is said will have to be recorded, but having a written record will prove useful, particularly on issues that are unresolved. A note taker who knows Russian will have two advantages. First, all Russian statements will be heard twice, once in the original Russian and again in English translation, thus giving the note taker more time to write and to be certain that what is recorded is correct. Second, nuances in Russian may not come through in the English translation.

When speaking through an interpreter, use simple words, short phrases, and no colloquial expressions or sports idioms. Pause frequently and signal to the interpreter when to proceed. Show signs of listening attentively to your Russian interlocutor, even if you do not understand what is said, and don't interrupt. Look at the speaker, not the interpreter. And don't preface your remarks with "Tell him that...." Speak directly to your interlocutor, not to the interpreter.

Interpreters vary in quality and consistency in both countries and can be a source of misunderstanding. It is always helpful to have someone on the U.S. side of the table who is conversant in Russian and can monitor the interpreting.

Patience is a Russian virtue that pays off in negotiations. When negotiating on their home turf, Russians can afford to wait out the other side. For you, however, time may be money, and Moscow is not the most pleasant city in which to while away costly hours. You may therefore be tempted to make concessions in order to reach agreement quickly and return home. Resist such temptations. Conversely, Russians negotiating in the United States may wish to expedite an agreement, particularly if they are spending their own money for hotel and other costs.

Who goes first? Russians traditionally prefer to know the other side's position before revealing their own. They may do this by accepting your draft in advance but pleading that their own is not yet ready to present in exchange. When Russians host a negotiation, they will usually invite the other side to speak first. There is no particular disadvantage in doing so if the general outline of what each side hopes to achieve is known or if there is a unanimity of views in advance.

Surprises should be avoided. If some radically new idea is to be proposed, discuss it with the Russians informally, in advance of the negotiations, thereby giving them time to study the proposal and prepare a response. When presented with a new and unexpected proposal at the negotiating table, Russians will have to retreat to a previous position and seek instructions from higher up. And as former U.S. ambassador to Moscow Llewellyn Thompson advised, "Don't maneuver the Russian bear into a corner from which there is no escape; in such a position he can become vicious."[*]

---

[*] From Thompson's final briefing for American correspondents prior to departure from Moscow in 1968, a meeting the author attended.

158

At the negotiating table the two drafts are compared, line by line, word for word. Wherever the language of the Russian and English drafts is identical or similar in meaning, agreement is reached and those paragraphs are set aside. Where the two drafts differ in substance, brackets are placed around the language in question to signify the differences that remain to be negotiated. A Russian offer to negotiate and reach agreement on each article of the drafts seriatim (individually and in succession) should be politely declined. Instead, the two drafts should first be reviewed in their entirety to identify all differences before the actual negotiating begins. This will permit some bracketed passages to be traded off against others.

When Russians make a concession—accepting the language of the U.S. draft—they will usually expect a corresponding concession in return, a quid pro quo in another part of the draft. Where such trade-offs occur, they should be of equal importance. Russians have been known to concede a minor point but then demand a major concession in exchange. To avoid this, agreement should be sought first on all minor differences between the two drafts. Major differences should be left to the final stage of the negotiation, the endgame.

Regarding concessions, negotiators should understand which side wants or needs the agreement more. That side, commonly referred to in French as the *demandeur*, would normally be expected to make more concessions.

Experienced negotiators will also include several "throwaways" in their draft. These are demands they know in advance the other side cannot accept. At some stage of the negotiation these may be withdrawn in exchange for concessions by the other side, which will have its own throwaways.

The Endgame

The Russian is patient until challenged.

—Russian proverb

The final stage of a negotiation, the endgame, is the most dramatic, similar to the final minutes of a close football game. The minor issues have been resolved, but one or more major differences is still outstanding. The score is tied, the clock is ticking, and one side or the other digs in for a goal-line stand.

Americans in such a situation, worn down by Russian patience and persistence, may be tempted to make concessions in order to end a lengthy negotiation and reach an agreement—which may be better than no agreement at all. But if the issues in dispute are important, you should resist that temptation. It should be made clear that further concessions cannot be made and that it would be better to have no agreement than a poor one. In the endgame Russians can be firm, but when challenged, they can also change positions radically if they want an agreement and are persuaded that the other side will not retreat.

When an impasse is reached, present your bottom line, those requirements that must be satisfied in order to agree. The Russians will appreciate this, but they will of course have their own bottom line. If there is to be an agreement, it must reflect the bottom lines of both sides.

In the endgame, agreement on differences can often be reached away from the negotiating table at a working lunch or during a break. The resolved issues should then be formally confirmed at the negotiating table. Russians are more difficult to draw out in a large forum with other Russians present. In a smaller group or, better still, one-on-one, they will often open up and reveal their innermost thoughts.

Russian negotiators may also have a personal, as well as an official, agenda. They may be concerned with promotion or demotion, personal advantage for themselves or their families, and the personal prestige resulting from a successful negotiation. If you can determine the nature of the negotiator's personal agenda, you will be better able to deal with it.

At times a negotiator is able to agree to a particular point but may not be certain that the home office—government, board of directors, or financial backers—will also agree. In such cases, agreement can be reached *ad referendum*, meaning that it is contingent upon agreement by higher authorities. For visitors to Moscow, this can usually be accomplished with a telephone call, fax, or e-mail to the home office. Bear in mind, though, that telephone communications may be monitored.

Beware of all-night sessions. To meet a deadline, there is often a temptation to continue negotiations through the night until an agreement has been hammered out. But such marathon meetings and the resulting fatigue can put undue pressure on one side or the other to capitulate or make concessions they may later regret. Better to sleep on the differences and start anew and refreshed the following morning.

The Paperwork

> Don't brag about the deal until you get the seal.
>
> —Russian proverb

Russians like to put agreements on paper, even on minor matters, duly signed by both parties, stating what has been agreed to and how it will be carried out. Even when formal agreement has not been reached, Russians will want to sign a *protokol*, a joint statement or memorandum of understanding, recording what has been discussed. The protokol is the Russian way, and it is almost impossible to avoid. Americans may wonder why they should sign something if no agreement has been reached. The protokol, however, can serve a useful purpose, for both sides, by providing a written record of what was discussed, what was agreed to, and what was not agreed to. For the Americans, it also shows that they negotiated in good faith. Moreover, the Russians may need a protokol to present to their higher-ups when they argue in favor of the agreement. Don't be afraid to sign one—the protokol has no legal force—but make sure you know what it says.

When agreement has finally been reached on all major issues, there is still much to be done. First, there is the usual cleanup work—small differences of substance in the English and Russian versions of the agreement, which usually turn up and must be smoothed out. Second, the English and Russian versions of the agreed language must be reconciled.

Agreements are customarily signed in two versions, English and Russian, both equally valid. But to do this, someone on the American side who is fluent in Russian must sit down with a Russian who is fluent in English and compare the two language versions to make certain that what they say and mean is identical. This is not easily done because, as we have seen, there are many expressions in one language for which there are no exact equivalents in the other. Major language differences can often be reconciled by minor changes in one language or the other.

To be avoided is the papering over of differences by saying that Americans will understand what is meant in English, and Russians will understand what is meant in Russian. Substantial differences will inevitably resurface during implementation of the agreement and become a source of discord between the two parties. Ambiguous language will be interpreted by each side in its own favor.

As any lawyer will advise, read agreements carefully before you sign, and make certain that all language in the agreement is crystal clear, especially who pays for what, a subject of importance to both sides.

And as lawyers will also advise, if the subject of the agreement is important or involves financial or legal obligations, ask a lawyer to review it before you sign, even if that means reaching agreement ad referendum, in other words, initialing the document rather than signing it, then signing later after the review has been completed.

Verification

A man is judged by his deeds, not his words.
                                                    —Russian proverb

Can Russians be trusted to honor commitments? The prudent

response to this question—and to many other questions about Russia—is "yes, but...."

According to Zbigniew Brzezinski, Anglo-Saxons and Russians have different concepts of trust:

> The Anglo-Saxons approach these issues like negotiated, legal agreements. It might be called a litigational approach. To the Russians, a commitment is binding as long as it is historically valid, so to speak. And its historical validity depends on the degree to which that commitment is either self-enforcing or still mutually advantageous. If it ceases to be self-enforcing or mutually advantageous, it obviously has lapsed. (1983)

To ensure that an agreement is observed, include a provision for regular review of implementation. This usually takes the form of periodic meetings between the two sides, held alternately in each country, to review past performance and make plans for the future. If such meetings are held, the agreement is more likely to be observed and not allowed to atrophy. As Ronald Reagan, recalling an old Russian proverb, repeatedly reminded former President Mikhail Gorbachev during their summit meetings, "Trust, but verify."

Related to verification are accountability and reporting, particularly when the expenditure of funds is involved. Russians can be notoriously lax about using funds effectively and about accounting for the expenditures, a problem recognized by Gorbachev.

One of perestroika's best-known slogans was *khozraschot*, usually translated as "cost accounting." The intent, however, was cost effectiveness, particularly in determining the real costs of producing goods and services. After sixty years of a command economy in which production costs were subsidized by the state, Russians have little experience in determining profit or loss. Under khozraschot, the objective was to make Russian enterprises self-sufficient by basing the prices of produced goods on true costs.

A related problem is accountability of donated funds. American donors to Russian cultural and philanthropic institutions have reported difficulties in obtaining prompt and detailed reporting on how their funds are being expended. Some new Russian foundations have scoffed at the standard regulatory and accounting procedures required by American donors. As one Russian foundation official put it, "We are all fine Christian men, and our [Russian] donors don't question what we do with their money" (Tennison 1990).

Such a response should not be seen as an intent to deceive but rather as an intercultural difference. Americans understand the need for accountability, annual financial reports, and audits by certified public accountants. But requesting such procedures from Russians may be seen as questioning their good faith and honesty. When encountering indignation over reporting requirements, Americans may wish to answer, "Trust, but verify."

Expect the Unexpected

> Russia is predictable in the sense that it will continue to be unpredictable.
> —Marshall Goldman

Things seldom go as planned with Russians. The will is there in most cases, but the bureaucracy is notoriously inefficient and its wheels turn slowly. A government that claims to give high priority to planning often inexplicably does things at the last minute and without a plan. And the best-laid plans may not be carried out as intended, even when details are spelled out in agreements that have been negotiated and signed in good faith.

"One of the most significant features of Russian behavior," wrote Wright Miller, an Englishman who lived many years in Russia,

> [is] that abandonment to the thing in hand which makes it difficult for so many Russians to keep regular habits unless they are obliged, which makes them careless of detailed preparation...yet capable of bouts of long-continued activity which are beyond the endurance of the ordinary Westerner. (1961, 90)

Russians will often say, "In principle, it can be done." But in practice, it often cannot. Russians begin discussions with generalities and leave the details to be dealt with later. In their enthusiasm to reach agreement, officials may exaggerate the possibilities by signing agreements and making promises that offer more than they are actually able to deliver.

Where should you start in picking up the pieces after an agreement has fallen apart? Throughout this book, much has been made of the importance of the personal factor in doing business in Russia, where people are often more important than machines or technology. For an agreement to be truly successful, there should be a personal relationship between an American on one side and a Russian on the other who are both committed to making something happen. When nothing happens—an agreement is not implemented—the American will have to return to the personal relationship. Reestablishing that relationship—by phone or preferably with another visit—can help piece things back together.

But things do happen without planning, as George H. W. Bush learned in May 1990 when Gorbachev, less than two weeks before his Washington Summit meeting with Bush, unexpectedly made public his plans to also visit Minneapolis and California. The announcement created turmoil in the White House because the Kremlin had not presented an itinerary for the proposed coast-to-coast tour, hotel rooms had not been reserved in Minneapolis or California, and no provisions had been made for Gorbachev's security or for supplying the special fuel needed for his Aeroflot jet. As *The New York Times* noted, "even the most rudimentary preparations have not been made for the kind of cross-country trek that the White House would spend months planning" (20 May 1990).

Failure to pin down details can also have unexpected consequences in cultural exchange. The first U.S.-Soviet cultural agreement, signed in 1958, provided for "sister university" relationships between universities in the two countries. Under the agreement, Indiana University (IU) was paired with Tashkent University.

The following year, a delegation from Tashkent arrived at IU in Bloomington, Indiana, without advance notice, on the Friday afternoon of a football weekend, when all nearby hotel and motel rooms had been reserved. To make matters worse, the Soviets were without funds because they had flown from New York City to Chicago and had then spent all their dollars for a taxi to Bloomington, *Illinois*—right city, wrong state. Moreover, the letter from Moscow announcing their arrival plans was received at IU after the delegation had completed its visit and returned home (Byrnes 1976, 62–63).

Thirty years later, in 1989, hilarious history repeated itself. Five Russian chefs in an exchange between U.S. and Russian food professionals were lost for five hours in the New York City area. The Russians had landed at Newark Airport, but their American hosts were awaiting them at Kennedy Airport, where they were expected to arrive. Nevertheless, the Russian and American chefs eventually found each other and were soon in the kitchen cooking things up together despite the misplaced arrival (Burros 1989).

Russians often don't comply with agreed-on timetables for action. Officials do not answer their mail promptly. The best way to finalize decisions or start-ups is through a face-to-face meeting, which, of course, can mean a trip to Russia and added expense.

But a trip to Novosibirsk once, for a face-to-face meeting, produced a surprise for an American from Minneapolis. After months of arranging his visit and confirming it by telex, as *The New York Times* reported, the man traveled halfway around the world to meet the Russian fellow expert in the Siberian city, only to discover on arrival that his Russian colleague was in Minneapolis. As explained by Susan Hartman, codirector of the Minneapolis group that arranged the Novosibirsk visit: "National organizations [in Russia] will disappear and reappear under different names with different people running them" (28 May 1990). Americans, who are usually sticklers for planning, should be prepared to expect the unexpected.

Government policies are suddenly and inexplicably changed and new initiatives are announced without adequate preparation, as President Bill Clinton learned in Budapest in December 1994 at a fifty-three-nation summit meeting on European security. At that meeting, according to *The New York Times*, Boris Yeltsin, after earlier agreeing to join NATO's Partnership for Peace, unexpectedly declared Russia's open opposition to the expansion of NATO into Central and Eastern Europe, adding caustically that "Europe is in danger of plunging into a cold peace" (6 December 1994). Four months later, Yeltsin's position changed again at his Moscow Summit with Clinton, where he agreed to Russia's joining the Partnership for Peace. And of course, the Russian position changed again in November 2001, when President Vladimir Putin, in his summit with President George W. Bush, signaled a new cooperative Russian approach to NATO.

What you *can* expect in meetings in Russia is traditional hospitality. The conference table will be laden with bottled water and soft drinks, cookies, and sweets. Tea or coffee will be served. When an agreement or contract is signed, the signatories can expect to raise a glass of champagne. A festive lunch or dinner for visitors will usually be held with the customary four courses—zakuski, soup, main course, dessert—and vodka and wine.

When Russians visit the United States, they expect the same treatment and are disappointed when their hospitality is not returned to the same degree. At the State Department, where funds for entertaining were negligible, we were always embarrassed when all we could offer our Russian visitors was coffee or tea in a Styrofoam cup. The Russians were initially impressed by the Styrofoam, which they had not seen before, but the novelty soon wore off. Americans who serve coffee or tea to Russians should be aware that drinks should always be served with something to eat, even if only a cookie.

7

Seeing the Real Russia

> They occupy your every moment; they distract your thoughts; they engross your attention; they tyrannize over you by means of officious politeness; they inquire how you pass your days; they question you with an importunity known only to themselves, and by fete after fete they prevent you seeing their country.
> —Marquis de Custine, *Empire of the Czar*

The Marquis de Custine's frustrations over Russian hospitality have been shared by many visitors since 1839. The Russian practice of keeping visitors occupied round the clock is an old one, and obsession with secrecy is often assumed to be the reason.

The KGB, to be sure, can still be expected to maintain its vigilance in protecting state secrets from the eyes of curious foreign visitors, but Russian hosts may still persist in filling every available hour of a visitor's time with sightseeing and other activities merely for the sake of hospitality.

The explanation lies in the seriousness with which Russians regard their obligations toward guests. *Gostepriimstvo* (hospitality) has a broader and deeper meaning in Russian than in English. In Russian it means overwhelming guests with food, drink, attention, and entertainment; total dedication to the guests' every need and comfort; and making certain that they are not bored.

Unfortunately, with such a busy schedule, visitors find it more difficult to see the real Russia. Your visit to Russia should include more than a Kremlin tour, the circus, the Hermitage Museum, and other obligatory tourist sights. You should try to learn how Russians live.

A department store is a good place to begin a city tour. Note the prices of the merchandise, but don't attempt to convert the prices to dollars. Try instead to figure out what an item would cost a Russian in terms of a monthly wage. Russian acquaintances will know what the average worker currently earns; don't hesitate to ask.

Visit a food store and food markets to see what is available, and note the prices. Check out the price of bread, a staple of the Russian diet. Flea markets, found in most cities, are also worth a visit, but watch out for pickpockets.

Railroad stations are a scene out of old Russia. Each day millions of visitors swarm into Moscow and other major cities by train. Most of the visitors are on foraging trips (from distances of up to a hundred miles) to buy items that are not available in their hometowns. If you will visit only Moscow or another large city, railroad stations provide an opportunity to see common people from small towns and villages as well as the *bomzhi* (homeless), who are kept off streets by the militsia. Also visible in the stations these days are many of the tens of thousands of homeless children—orphans and runaways from broken homes or dysfunctional families—who roam the streets of Moscow and other large cities, subsisting on begging, petty theft, and handouts from soup kitchens and charitable organizations.

All of Moscow's railroad stations are accessible via the Metro (subway). The Leningrad, Kazan, and Yaroslavl Stations are conveniently located adjacent to each other at the Komsomolskaya Metro Station. (Yes, in Moscow it's still called the Leningrad Station.) Be sure to check out the Russians outside the railroad stations, as well as Metro stations and public markets, selling everything from family heirlooms and used clothing to homemade food products for a few rubles to supplement their meager incomes. But be cautious in buying food from street vendors, especially meat products and alcohol; they may not be good for your health.

The Metro is also a good place to "people watch," and although the fare has increased, it's still the best buy in town. With its more than 150 stations and a network of 150 miles, the Moscow Metro can take you anywhere you want to go and is a model of efficiency. Moreover, travel underground is much faster than surface travel because traffic jams can be massive and cause lengthy delays. The Metro carries 18 million passengers on an average workday and is very crowded during rush hour, but trains run every 90 seconds during rush hour and every 2 to 4 minutes during the rest of the day. Tokens can be purchased for single trips, plastic cards for a number of trips. Route maps are available and will make the Metro easier to use. Metros in other large Russian cities are comparable.

Churches offer another glimpse of old Russia as well as an opportunity to see the growing interest in things Russian and things spiritual. Of the 77,676 Russian Orthodox churches that existed before the Revolution, only a few thousand survived communist persecution. Many have now reopened and are well worth a visit.

Street crime, which rose sharply during the early 1990s, has now leveled off and is less than in many major U.S. cities. Nevertheless, foreigners are still targeted, and some precautions are advised. Don't call attention to yourself. Try not to stand out or look like a tourist. Leave expensive jewelry at home. Wear plain clothing. Buy a Russian hat and wear it. Don't wear fancy shoes, a sure giveaway. Speak softly, try to blend in, and take the same precautions you would in Rome, New York City, or London.

Beware of underground passages, which are often the scene of robberies. Protect yourself against pickpockets in crowds and in the Metro, and be on guard against the bands of street urchins who surround tourists and deftly relieve them of their valuables. Wear a money belt, and carry only small amounts of currency. Keep in your pockets only what you need for that day so you don't have to pull out a big wad of bills to make a purchase. If you give money to one beggar, you will soon be surrounded by many others with outstretched hands. And keep somewhere in a safe place a copy of the page of your passport that contains your photo, passport number, and date and place of issuance. It will expedite getting a replacement at your country's nearest consulate if your passport is lost or stolen.

Look down, not up, and watch your step. Russian streets are full of potholes and other obstacles, and sidewalks have a habit of unexpectedly dropping off. And in winter, watch out for falling icicles big enough to cause serious injury to pedestrians on the sidewalks below.

Traffic is supposed to stop for pedestrians but does not always do so, even in designated crosswalks, and drivers run red lights when they believe they can get away with it. Do not cross streets against traffic lights. Carry a small pocket flashlight at night. If you use taxis, negotiate the price before beginning your ride, and do not share rides with strangers. If traveling overnight by train, keep your compartment door locked. Keep your passport and visa with you at all times, in an inside pocket; the militsia makes random checks of identity documents, and if you don't have yours, you may be fined or have to pay a bribe to be let off. Drink only bottled water, which is always available, and use it to brush your teeth.

The real Russia can be found in the many smaller cities, towns, and villages, where the bulk of the population lives, many of them in areas formerly closed to travel by foreign visitors. These formerly closed cities, isolated for many years from the rest of the world because they were centers of military-industrial production, are the traditional Russia. The pace of life is slower, people are more polite, and Western influence is less evident. In 1992, in Saratov, a large industrial city on the Volga River, I met with English teachers at the high school and university level who told me that I was the first native English speaker they had ever encountered. Such cities, now emerging from their previous isolation, are becoming increasingly important as political and economic power devolves from Moscow to the provinces. And it is in the provinces that the real political pulse of Russia can be taken.

For a glimpse of old Russia, a village visit is also a must. The contrast between urban and rural life in Russia and America has been noted by writer Vassily Aksyonov:

> America's prosperity becomes apparent the moment you leave her large cities. In Russia the opposite is the case. What remains after the military has drained off most of the resources goes toward maintaining a minimal level of decency in the cities; the countryside and the villages are left to rot. (1989, 30)

A somewhat different view of Russian villages is given by Serge Schmemann, *The New York Times* correspondent, who in 1990, after many attempts, finally received permission from the Soviet authorities to visit the ancestral home of his gentry forebears, ninety miles south of Moscow:

> The more I visited Sergiyevskoye, the more it enchanted me. The mud was treacherous, the winters pitiless, the backwardness and inefficiency appalling, but the landscape was that timeless collage of birches, meadows, log cabins, and rivers of which Pushkin wrote, "It smells of Russia here." (1997, 51)

8

Whither Russia?

> Whenever the right of speech shall be restored to this muzzled people, the astonished world will hear so many disputes arise, that it will believe the confusion of Babel again returned.
> —Marquis de Custine, *Empire of the Czar*

With free speech restored, the new Russia is indeed a Babel of disputes, as foreseen by the Marquis de Custine in 1839. But as Russians seek to develop a democracy and civil society, the disputes are far from civil and are better described as *skloka* (squabble).

"*Skloka* is a phenomenon born of our social order....," wrote Olga Freidenberg, a cousin of Boris Pasternak. As she explained,

> Skloka stands for base, trivial hostility, unconscionable spite breeding petty intrigues, the vicious pitting of one clique against another. It thrives on calumny, informing, spying, scheming, slander, the igniting of base passions.... Skloka is the alpha and omega of our politics. Skloka is our method. (1982, 303–304)

In the early years of the twenty-first century, Russians are still squabbling. Absent a culture of compromise, everyone takes sides. Westernizers squabble with Slavophiles, liberals with conservatives, reformers with traditionalists, democrats with democrats, communists with all of the above, and all of this takes place in

173

a country with no tradition of political coalition building. The squabbling, moreover, is steeped in insults and abuse.

"In other countries," writes Pavel Palazchenko, former Presdient Mikhail Gorbachev's English interpreter and foreign policy aide, "people argue in order to find the truth. In this country you argue in order to prove that you are one hundred percent right and to destroy your opponent" (1997, 153). Or, as Gorbachev more diplomatically put it, "we are an emotional people, we lack the culture to conduct debate and respect the viewpoint even of a friend, a comrade" (*Pravda*, 15 July 1987).

Today's squabbling has roots in the Soviet past, says sociologist Dmitri Shalin.

> The emotional abuse that Russian intellectuals casually heap on each other these days is a sure sign that their predecessors were themselves abused. All those who survived Stalinist purges, intimidation by the KGB, or ideologically inspired violence of any kind could not help being deeply troubled by their experiences. (1995, 19)

Indeed, the older generation is confused, frightened, less inclined to support change, and more likely to support the communists. And their confusion and fear are understandable.

"Few nations," writes *The New York Times* correspondent Serge Schmemann, "have followed a historical trail quite as erratic, careening from feudalism to Brave New World, total war, famine, global might, and finally collapse, all in the span of one average lifetime" (26 December 1993).

Less affected by this troubled past is the younger generation. Better educated than its elders, knowing more about Russia and the rest of the world, more receptive to change, and with the optimism and energy of youth, this generation has greater hopes and expectations for the future. Moreover, these eighteen to thirty-year-olds constitute the wealthiest and most dynamic demographic group in Russian society today. "Out of all social groups," says Yuri Levada, Russia's most respected pollster, "young people are the richest, the most well-off. They have bigger salaries and they don't have families yet or responsibilities. They know how to earn money, and their salaries are the largest." But in addition to their materialism and lack of interest in politics, Levada also notes their "total absence of any larger ideas or values which you usually find in this segment of the population. They have no concept about any long-lasting values in life" (2001).

Adding to Russia's travails is its decline as a great power, and exacerbating that decline is a demographic downturn. In 1992, there were 148.3 million Russians, but by July of 2002 only 145 million, and the decrease is accelerating. If the current birth and death rates continue, Russian demographers project a further decline to slightly more than 134 million in 2016 (*RIA Novosti*, 16 May 2002).

In most developed countries, population decline is due to a low birthrate; in Russia, however, the low birthrate is combined with a high death rate. In fact, the nation's death rate is nearly double its birthrate. Moreover, the reproduction rate (the number of births a woman has), as reported by the *Christian Science Monitor*, decreased from 1.7 in 1991 to 1.1 in 2002, much less than the 2.4 needed to stabilize the population (18 April 2002). Moreover, only 40 percent of newborns are considered healthy.

One radical idea to reverse the declining birthrate, proposed by far-right deputy Vladimir Zhirinovsky, was to legalize polygamy. Zhirinovsky's preposterous proposal was rejected by the Duma, but as Islam allows a man to have four wives, the chairman of the Russia's Council of Muftis, Ravil Gainutdin, endorsed it as a way to halt the demographic decline (*RFE/RL*, 19 October 2001).

Life expectancy has also declined. In 2002, as reported in the *Christian Science Monitor*, it was 72 for women and 59 for men (18 April 2002). By comparison, life expectancy in the United States in 2001 was a record-high 80 for women and 74.4 for men. In the United Kingdom, estimated life expectancy in 2001 was 80.6 for women and 77.8 for men.

Particularly worrisome is the high death rate for people of working age. Half of Russian deaths in the 1990s were caused by cardiovascular diseases, with second place held not by cancer, as elsewhere in industrial countries, but by accidents and injuries as well as murders, suicides, and alcohol poisoning. These latter three factors were involved in half of the deaths among working-age men.

Contributing to these dire demographics are excessive use of alcohol and tobacco, poor nutrition, lower standards of sanitation, unhealthy working conditions and lifestyles, environmental degradation, deterioration of health-care delivery systems, and a resultant return of infectious and other diseases. In recent years, Russia has suffered outbreaks of typhus, typhoid fever, and cholera. Drug-resistant tuberculosis has more than doubled since 1990. The incidence of syphilis has skyrocketed, and drug abuse has caused alarming increases in AIDS and hepatitis. Travelers to Russia should mind their behavior and be sure that their immunizations are up-to-date.

But as the health of Russians has deteriorated, the health of the economy has improved as painful reforms have begun to show results. By 2002 industrial and agricultural production was up, personal income had risen along with domestic demand, a market for consumer goods was developing, and the trade balance was favorable. Crude oil, natural gas, and minerals provided a steady stream of foreign currency. A middle class was emerging, and the well-being of many Russians had improved. Problems remained, however, with the manufacturing sector, where nearly half the industries were simply not competitive in international markets but could not be closed because entire regions depended on them for employment and the services they provided to their employees. Moreover, much of the Russian recovery, as well as its future, was based on the unpredictable price of oil and minerals on the world market.

As a consequence, the country remains divided between haves and have-nots, winners and losers in the privatization process. Among the haves is a phenomenon called "crony capitalism" in which interlocking networks of business and government officials, many with familiar faces from the communist nomenklatura, maintain monopolies and originate oligopolies. Among the have-nots are pensioners and others on fixed incomes who have been impoverished by inflation. More than one in four Russians lives in poverty, and rampant crime affects both the haves and have-nots. It is little wonder that many Russians, humiliated by their loss of empire and superpower status, are also embittered and demoralized by the decline in their living standard in so short a time span.

As a result, there is nostalgia for the economic stability and personal safety of the Brezhnev years. More than half of all Russians are said to believe that life was better before 1991, when the Soviet Union broke up. A public opinion poll taken in January 2000 testified to the enormous staying power of various aspects of the Soviet worldview. As Timothy Colton and Michael McFaul put it in their study of the poll results,

> In all age groups the most appealing system for Russians was either a reformed Soviet system or, for those seventy or older, an unreconstructed Soviet-style regime...the longer a Russian lived with the Soviet dictatorship, the more likely he or she is to have clung to Soviet political values. (2001, 17)

Conversely, however, younger Russians are more indifferent to the breakup of the Soviet Union, and any nostalgia they may have had for the past is fading fast. In a poll taken in 2001, 55 percent of respondents preferred life before the reforms. Two years earlier, that figure was 64 percent (*Vremya Novostei* [Moscow], 2001).

And yet, despite Russia's troubles, there is tranquility in the streets as Russians hunker down and endure, as they have so often in the past. Food and consumer goods have become more expensive, but Russians no longer have to stand in long lines to make their purchases. And as in the past, Russians have drawn on their agricultural heritage and are producing in their small private or communal gardens much of the food they consume.

Reforms are under way that are independent of current political leaders. Privatization is proceeding, although many of the former state-owned factories are still run by the same directors, and in the same way as in the past, by their old managers and with old machinery. Western advisers had assumed that introduction of a free market would automatically result in Western-style institutions. But as Zbigniew Fallenbuchl, a Canadian economist, comments,

> We know that it is difficult to change the behavior of managers in industry. Often it does not make much difference whether the enterprise is still state-owned, has been commercialized, or even really privatized. Despite changed objective conditions it is always easier to make decisions in the old familiar way. You have to "unlearn" the way the enterprises were run in the past in order to accept new criteria and methods. (1977, 48)

Russia has an elected president and parliament, and the parliament is independent, although subordinate to the president. Voter turnout for elections is high—more than 60 percent—higher than in the United States. A civil society is emerging in a country where, until recently, the government ran everything. Some 350,000 nongovernmental organizations have been registered by the Ministry of Justice, and 70,000 are considered to be operational and providing assistance to twenty million Russians (Arkhangelsky 2001). They represent independent civic action groups that work on such diverse issues as human rights, health, labor, small business, child rights, anticonscription, ethnicity, and many other causes that could not have been openly championed in the Soviet Union. The pace and scope of reform may be questioned, but the process seems irreversible, although most informed observers believe it will take a generation or more to complete.

Some Western analysts question whether Russia still qualifies as a great power, and they consider the nation to be geopolitically irrelevant. Others, however, note that Russia is geographically the largest country in the world; it is strategically located at the center of the Eurasian land mass; and it has enormous natural resources, a nuclear arsenal, the largest pool of scientists and engineers, an educated middle class, a literate and skilled workforce, and a seat on the United Nations Security Council. Looking back on their long history, Russians are indeed persuaded that they are a great power, and they want to be seen as a major player on the world stage.

Russia's first contacts with the West, in the early eighteenth century, began a long and slow process of Europeanization that led to a flowering of creativity in the nineteenth century—the Silver Age, as it is called—in literature, music, and art. Contacts with the West also led to cautious attempts at reform of state and society. A second burst of creativity and reform occurred during the 1920s, following the Revolution and a civil war that destroyed the old order but released the latent talent and creativity of the Russians and other nationalities in the multiethnic state.

Unfortunately, the Silver Age was followed by social and political unrest, a world war, revolution, Stalin's terror, and a new ideology, Marxism-Leninism, which stifled the creativity and reforms of the 1920s. It is not unfair, therefore, to question what Russians will do this time with their newfound freedoms and renewed contacts with the West.

Russia has a new president, Vladimir Putin, who is young, healthy, energetic, does not drink or smoke, and believes that his country's future is with the West. Putin, a former KGB officer, has appointed many of his former KGB colleagues to senior positions and is giving Russia some much-needed direction. He has been criticized for his authoritarian style and his government's increasing control of the media, but his decision to support the United States in its war on terrorism, his interest in developing a partnership with NATO, and his agreement with President George W. Bush for a radical reduction in the two countries' nuclear warheads indicate a desire to work more closely with the West and its leading power, the U.S. These are indeed momentous changes, but it is fair to ask if they are permanent, and if so, will they also change Russia?

In answering such a question, George F. Kennan has counseled, "Whatever happens...Russia is, and is going to remain, a country very different from our own. We should not look for this difference to be overcome in any short space of time" (1989, 58).

Whatever Russia emerges from this time of turmoil, history tells us that it will be influenced by the same forces that have shaped the country in the past—geography, history, culture, religion, and governance. The new state will be neither European nor Asian, but uniquely Russian, and the capacity of the West to affect the outcome will be marginal.

As Harold Berman once wrote, "The Soviet rulers are not the ultimate masters of Russia's fate; on the contrary, Russia is the ultimate master of their fate" (1963, 269).

The same can be said of Russia's rulers today.

Afterword

Russia has often been too much for the Russians themselves—
there has been just too much space, too much winter, too much
suffering, too much bureaucracy, meanness, aspiration. It can certainly be too much for a visitor, no matter how sympathetic.
—Alfred Kazin, *Russian Sketches*

Human nature and national spirit cannot be changed overnight,
especially by force. One can only hope to facilitate their internal
processes.
—Fedor Burlatsky, "War of Civilizations? Never!"

Selected Bibliography

Afanasyev, Yuri. 1991. "The Coming Dictatorship." *New York Review of Books*, 31 January.

Aksyonov, Vassily. 1989. *In Search of Melancholy Baby*. Translated by Michael Henry Heim and Antonina W. Bouis. New York: Random House, Vintage Books.

Albats, Yevgenia. 2001. *Moscow Times*, 20 December.

Amalryk, Andrei. 1982. *Notes of a Revolutionary*. Translated by Guy Daniels. New York: Knopf.

Arkhangelsky, Alexander. 2001. "Civil Society Is Being Born in Russia." *JRL* 5559, 21 November.

Åslund, Anders. 2002. *Building Capitalism: The Transformation of the Former Soviet Bloc*. New York: Cambridge University Press.

Baryshnikov, Mikhail. In *Parade Magazine*, 8 October 1989.

Belyakov, Vladimir, and Walter J. Raymond, eds. 1994. *The Constitution of the Russian Federation*. Lawrenceville, VA: Brunswick Publishing.

Berdyaev, Nikolai. 1960. *The Origin of Russian Communism*. Ann Arbor: University of Michigan Press.

Berman, Harold J. 1963. *Justice in the U.S.S.R.* Rev. ed. Cambridge: Harvard University Press.

Billington, James H. 1970. *The Ikon and the Axe: An Interpretive History of Russian Culture*. New York: Random House, Vintage Books.

Brown, Archie, and Lilia Shevtsova, eds. 2001. *Gorbachev, Yeltsin, and Putin: Political Leadership in Russia's Transition*. Washington, DC: Carnegie Endowment for International Peace.

Brzezinski, Zbigniew. 1983. Interview with Radio Liberty-Radio Free Europe. In *The Wall Street Journal*, 25 March.

Burros, Marian. 1989. "5 Russians Skirmish with a U.S. Kitchen and Everyone Wins." *The New York Times*, 19 July.

Byrnes, Robert F. 1976. *Soviet-American Academic Exchanges, 1958–1975*. Bloomington: Indiana University Press.

Carnaghan, Ellen, and Donna Bahry. 1994. "Feminism and Democratization in the Post-Soviet Transition." Paper presented at the annual meeting of the American Association for the Advancement of Slavic Studies. Philadelphia, PA, 18 November.

Chekhov, Anton. *Three Sisters*, Act II.

Chukovsky, Kornei. 1984. *The Art of Translation*. Translated by Lauren G. Leighton. Knoxville: University of Tennessee Press.

Cohen, Stephen F. 1985. *Rethinking the Soviet Experience*. New York: Oxford University Press.

Colton, Timothy J., and Michael McFaul. 2001. *Are Russians Undemocratic?* Washington, DC: The Carnegie Endowment for International Peace, Working Paper No. 30 (June).

Connell, Rachel. 1991. In *Crossways*, newsletter of the American Collegiate Consortium for East-West Cultural and Academic Exchange. Middlebury, VT (Spring).

Constitution (Fundamental Law) of the Union of Soviet Socialist Republics. 1977. Moscow: Novosti.

Custine, Marquis de. 1989. *Empire of the Czar: A Journey through Eternal Russia*. New York: Doubleday, Anchor Books.

DaVanzo, Julie, and Clifford Grammich. 2001. *Dire Demographics: Population Trends in the Russian Federation*. Santa Monica, CA: The Rand Corporation.

Department of State, *Background Note—Russia*. http://www.state.gov/r/pa/bgn/index.cfm?docid=3183.

Eklof, Ben, and Edward Dneprov, eds. 1993. *Democracy in the Russian School: The Reform Movement in Education Since 1984*. Boulder, CO: Westview Press.

Fallenbuchl, Zbigniew M. 1977. "'Unlearning' and the Process of Transition." In *ALMANAC(H)*, edited by Marie Lavigne. Pau, France, self-published.

Feshbach, Murray. 1995. *Ecological Disaster: Cleaning Up the Hidden Legacy of the Soviet Regime*. New York: Twentieth Century Fund.

———. 1994. Talk at Kennan Institute, Washington, DC, 1 November; and in conversations with the author.

———. 1989. Testimony at hearing, "A Changing Soviet Society," before Commission on Security and Cooperation in Europe, CSCE 101, 17 May. Washington, DC: U.S. Government Printing Office.

Field, Mark G. 1994. "Postcommunist Medicine: Morbidity, Mortality, and the Deteriorating Health Situation." In *The Social Legacy of Communism*, edited by James A. Millar and Sharon L. Wolchik. Washington, DC, and New York: Woodrow Wilson Center Press and Cambridge University Press.

Freidenberg, Olga. 1982. In *The Correspondence of Boris Pasternak and Olga Freidenberg, 1910–1954*, by Elliot Mossman. New York: Harcourt Brace Jovanovitch.

Geyer, Georgie Ann. 1990. "Wrong Basket?" *Washington Times*, 31 May.

Gilbert, Martin. 1993. *Atlas of Russian History*. 2d ed. New York: Oxford University Press.

Gisse, Yves. 1997. "Valeurs culturelles traditionelles et transition economique." In *ALMANAC(H)*, edited by Marie Lavigne. Pau, France, self-published.

Goldman, Marshall. 1995. "Comrade Godfather." *Washington Post*, 12 February.

———. 1990. "Gorbachev at Risk." *World Monitor*, June.

Gorbachev, Mikhail. 1989. Address to Parliamentary Assembly, Council of Europe, Strasbourg, France (6 July).

———. 1987. *Perestroika: New Thinking for Our Country and the World*. New York: Harper & Row.

———. 1987. Speech to cultural and media executives, Pravda, 15 July.

186

Havel, Vaclav. 1990. Acceptance speech on receiving Peace Prize of German Booksellers Association, 15 October 1989. Translated by A. G. Brain. *New York Review of Books*, 18 January.

Hayter, Sir William. 1966. *The Kremlin and the Embassy*. London: Hodder and Stoughton.

Henze, Paul B. 1987. In "Marx on Russians and Muslims." *Central Asian Survey* 6, no. 4.

Heller, Mikhail, and Aleksandr M. Nekrich. 1986. *Utopia in Power: The History of the Soviet Union from 1917 to the Present*. Translated by Phyllis B. Carlos. New York: Summit Books.

Hingley, Ronald. 1977. *The Russian Mind*. New York: Charles Scribner's Sons.

———. 1962. "That's No Lie, Comrade." *Problems of Communism* 11, no. 2.

Hosking, Geoffrey. 2001. *Russia and the Russians*. Cambridge: Harvard University Press.

———. 1990. *The Awakening of the Soviet Union*. Cambridge: Harvard University Press.

Hunt, Anna. 2001. "So Has the Russian Mafia Met Its Match?" *The Independent* (UK), November.

Kaiser, Robert G. 2001. *Washington Post Book World*, 8–14 July, T3.

Keenan, Edward. 1985. Lecture at Kennan Institute, Washington, DC, 24 September 1985, and interview with the author, 27 March 1996.

Keller, Bill. 1990. "Yearning for an Iron Hand." *The New York Times Magazine*, 28 January.

Kennan, George F. 1989. "After the Cold War." *The New York Times Magazine*, 5 February.

———. 1967. *Memoirs, 1925–1950*. Boston: Little, Brown.

Khrushcheva, Nina. 2000/2001. "Culture Matters, But Not (of All Places) in Russia." In *Correspondence: An International Review of Culture and Society*. Council on Foreign Relations, no. 7 (Winter).

Klose, Eliza K. 1994. *Surviving Together* 12 (Autumn).

Kohn, Hans, ed. 1955. *The Mind of Modern Russia*. New Brunswick, NJ: Rutgers University Press.

Laurinciukas, Albertas. 1977. "How I Failed to Find the Average American." In *Soviet Writers Look at America*, edited by Akexander Fursenko. Moscow: Progress Publishers.

Lenin, V. I. 1943. *Selected Works*. New York: International Publishers.

Levada, Yuri. 2001. "Russia: Nation's Youth Are Apolitical and Materialistic." Quoted by Jeremy Bransten, Moscow: RFE/RL, 7 November.

Lourie, Richard. 1991. *Predicting Russia's Future*. Knoxville, TN: Whittle Direct Books.

Lourie, Richard, and Aleksei Mikhalev. 1989. "Why You'll Never Have Fun in Russian." *New York Times Book Review*, 18 June.

Malia, Martin. 1961. "What Is the Intelligentsia?" In *The Russian Intelligentsia*, edited by Richard Pipes. New York: Columbia University Press.

Marsland, Richard. 2001. "At Risk of Losing a Wild Reputation: Russia." *Financial Times*, 4 April.

Mcculloch, William. 1994. Lecture at Kennan Institute. Washington, DC, 14 March.

McDaniel, Tim. 1996. *The Agony of the Russian Idea*. Princeton, NJ: Princeton University Press.

Mehnert, Klaus. 1961. *Soviet Man and His World*. New York: Frederick A. Praeger.

Miliukov, Paul. 1960. In *Outline of Russian Culture, Part I, Religion and the Church*, edited by Michael Karpovich. New York: A. S. Barnes.

Miller, Wright. 1961. *Russians as People*. New York: E. P. Dutton.

Monahan, Barbara. 1983. *A Dictionary of Russian Gesture*. Tenafly, NJ: Hermitage.

Morath, Inge, and Arthur Miller. 1969. *In Russia*. New York: Viking.

Palazchenko, Pavel. 1997. *My Years with Gorbachev and Shevardnadze: The Memoir of a Soviet Interpreter*. University Park: Pennsylvania State University Press.

Palmieri, Deborah Anne, ed. 2002. *The Ultimate Insider's Guide to Doing Business with Russia*, 2 vols. Washington, DC: Russian-American Chamber of Commerce.

Pearson, Landon. 1990. *Children of Glasnost: Growing Up Soviet.* Seattle: University of Washington Press.

Pipes, Richard. 1981. *U.S.-Soviet Relations in the Era of Détente.* Boulder, CO: Westview Press.

Poltavchenko, Georgi. 2000. *Rossiskaya Gazeta* (Moscow), 5 August.

Post, Laurens van der. 1965. *Journey Into Russia.* Harmondsworth, England: Penguin Books.

Prosterman, Roy L. et al. 1994. *Russian Agrarian Reform: A Status Report From the Field.* Seattle: Rural Development Institute.

Protzman, Ferdinand. 1989. "2 German-Soviet Pacts Called Vital First Steps." *The New York Times,* 15 June.

Putin, Lyudmila. 2001. "Ljudmila Staunt." *Der Spiegel* (Germany), 19 February.

Rahr, Alexander. 2000. *Wladimir Putin: Der Deutsche im Kreml.* Muenchen: Universitas.

Reddaway, Peter, and Dmitri Glinski. 2002. *The Tragedy of Russia's Reforms: Market Bolshevism Against Democracy.* Washington, DC: U.S. Institute of Peace.

Remnick, David. 1992. "The Trial of the Old Regime." *New Yorker* (30 November).

Richardson, Paul E. 1997. *Russia Survival Guide: Business and Travel.* Montpelier, VT: Russian Information Services.

Roosa, Ruth Amende. 1963. "Russian Industrialists Look to the Future: Thoughts on Economic Development, 1906–1917." In *Essays in Russian and Soviet History,* edited by John Shelton Curtiss. New York: Columbia University Press.

Rosenthal, Bernice Glatzer, ed. 1997. *The Occult in Russian and Soviet Culture.* Ithaca: Cornell University Press.

Rostropovich, Mstislav. 1990. "Soldiers of Music: Rostropovich Returns to Russia." PBS television film.

Schmemann, Serge, 1997. *Echoes of a Native Land: Two Centuries of a Russian Village.* New York: Alfred A. Knopf.

Seton-Watson, Hugh. 1952. *The Decline of Imperial Russia, 1855–1914.* New York: Frederick A. Praeger.

Shalin, Dmitri N., ed. 1995. *Russian Culture at the Crossroads: Paradoxes of Post-Communist Consciousness*. Boulder, CO: Westview Press.

Shishkin, Sergei. 1994. Talk at Kennan Institute, Washington DC, 25 October.

Shulman, Marshall. 1989. "Face-to-Face" lecture at Carnegie Endowment for International Peace, Washington, DC, 12 February.

Simis, Konstantin M. 1982. *USSR: The Corrupt Society*. New York: Simon & Schuster.

Sinyavsky, Andrei [Abram Tertz]. 1965. "Thought Unaware." *New Leader*, 48, no. 15 (19 July).

Smith, Hedrick. 1976. *The Russians*. New York: Times Books, Quadrangle.

Solomon, Peter H. Jr. 2001. "Fixing the Courts in Russia? The Putin/Kozak Reforms of 2001." Cambridge, MA: Cambridge Energy Research Associates.

Solomon, Peter H. Jr., and Todd S. Foglesong. 2000. *Courts and Transition in Russia*. Boulder, CO: Westview Press.

Solzhenitsyn, Aleksandr. 1975. *The Oak and the Calf: Sketches of Literary Life in the Soviet Union*. New York: Harper and Row.

Stites, Richard. 1991. Interview with author, 11 February.

———. 1989. *Revolutionary Dreams, Utopian Vision and Experimental Life in the Russian Revolution*. New York: Oxford University Press.

Sutherland, Jeanne. 1999. *Schooling in the New Russia: Innovation and Change, 1984–1995*. London and New York: Macmillan and St. Martin's Press.

Szamuely, Tibor. 1974. *The Russian Tradition*. New York: McGraw-Hill.

Talbott, Strobe. 2002. *The Russia Hand: A Memoir of Presidential Diplomacy*. New York: Random House.

Tatko, Amy. 1993. Article in *Crossways*, newsletter of the American Collegiate Consortium for East-West Cultural and Academic Exchange, Middlebury, VT (Spring).

Tennison, Sharon. 1990. Center for U.S.-U.S.S.R. Initiatives, San Francisco. Memo to U.S. foundations, 15 May.

Thom, Françoise. 1994. "Eurasianism: A New Russian Foreign Policy." *Uncaptive Minds* 7, no. 2 (Summer).

Tolstaya,Tatyana.1990. "Notes from the Underground." Translated by Jamey Gambell. *New York Review of Books*, 31 May.

Vakar, Nicholas P. 1962. *The Taproot of Soviet Society.* New York: Harper and Brothers.

van der Post, Laurens. 1965. *Journey into Russia.* Harmondworth, England: Penguin Books.

Vasko, Tibor. 1997. "Some Thoughts on Transformation by a Retired System Practitioner." In *ALMANAC(H)*, edited by Marie Lavigne. Pau, France, self-published.

Vernadsky, George. 1953. *The Mongols and Russia.* New Haven, CT: Yale University Press.

Visson, Lynn. 1998. *Wedded Strangers: The Challenges of Russian-American Marriages.* New York: Hippocrene Books.

Vremya Novostei (Moscow). 2001. In JRL 5586, 7 December.

Webber, Stephen L. 2000. *School, Reform and Society in the New Russia.* London and New York: Macmillan and St. Martin's Press.

Weil, Irwin. 1991. Interview with the author, 4 February.

Wortman, Richard S. 1976. *The Development of a Russian Legal Consciousness.* Chicago: University of Chicago Press.

Zernov, Nicolas. 1978. *The Russians and Their Church.* Crestwood, NY: St. Vladimir¹s Seminary Press.

Index

leveling, *see uravnilovka*
Levine, Irving, R., 143
Liberal Democratic Party, 67–68
Litvak, Lilya, 56
Lourie, Richard, 41, 44, 131, 139

M

mafia, 81, 82–84
Makarenko, Anton, 101
Malia, Martin, 96
Marx, Karl, 12, 124
Matuszewski, Daniel, 16
McCulloch, William, 113
McDonald's, 52–53
McFaul, Michael, 32, 177
messianism, 61–63
Metro, Moscow, 169
Mikhalev, Aleksei, 44, 139
militsia, 17, 97, 112, 126, 168, 170
Miliukov, Paul, 29
Miller, Arthur, 110, 118
Miller, Wright, 163
mir, 15, 16, 17, 18, 36–37, 65, 88–89, 92
mir i druzhba, 122
misunderstandings, 138–40
Moldovans, 23
Molotov, Vyacheslav, 152
Mongols, *see* Tatars
Morath, Inge, 110, 118
Moscow, 8, 11, 110, 143
Mother Russia, 52, 55
Muslim, *see* Islam

P

R

Rahr, Alexander, 95
Reagan, Ronald, 162
rebellion, 63–65
Rechtsstaat, 91, 92
religion, 23, 26–33
Reformation, 7
Remnick, David, 141
Renaissance, 7
revolt, 63–65
Roman Catholic, 23, 29, 32
Rome, 7
Roosa, Ruth, 38
Rostropovich, Mstislav, 45
"Russian idea," 66, 74
Russian language, 135–38
Russian soul, *see dusha*

S

Sakharov, Andrei, 50
Savitsky, Pyotr, 67
Schmemann, Serge, 61, 98, 171, 174
schools, *see* education
serfdom, 17
Seton-Watson, Hugh, 65, 74
Shalin, Dmitri N., 174
Shishkin, Sergei, 76
Shulman, Marshall, 41
Siberia, xxi, 11, 12, 37, 44, 54, 58, 96, 111, 147, 165
Silver Age, 179